PENGUIN BOOKS

A ZOO IN MY LUGGAGE

Gerald Durrell was born in Jamshedpur, India, in 1925. In 1928 his family returned to England and in 1933 they went to live on the Continent. Eventually they settled on the island of Corfu, where they lived until 1939. During this time he made a special study of zoology, and kept a large number of the local wild animals as pets. In 1945 he joined the staff of Whipsnade Park as a student keeper. In 1947 he financed, organized, and led his first animal-collecting expedition to the Cameroons. This was followed by a second expedition in 1948 and a third in 1949, this time to British Guiana. He has also made expeditions to Paraguay, Sierra Leone and Argentina. In 1962 he and his wife went to New Zealand, Australia, and Malaya to film a T.V. series, *Two in the Bush*, in conjunction with the B.B.C. Natural History Film Unit. In 1958 he founded the Jersey Zoological Park, of which he is the director, and in 1964 he founded the Jersey Wildlife Preservation Trust. Gerald Durrell's other books include *Menagerie Manor*, *The Bafut Beagles*, *My Family and Other Animals*, *Encounters With Animals*, *The Drunken Forest*, *Three Singles to Adventure* and *The Whispering Land* (all available in Penguins), and *The Overloaded Ark*.

His latest books are *Birds, Beasts and Relatives* (1969), *Fillets of Plaice,* and *Catch Me a Colubus* (1972).

GERALD DURRELL

A ZOO IN MY LUGGAGE

WITH ILLUSTRATIONS BY

Ralph Thompson

PENGUIN BOOKS

Penguin Books Ltd, Harmondsworth, Middlesex, England
Penguin Books Australia Ltd, Ringwood, Victoria, Australia

—

First published by Rupert Hart Davis, 1960
Published in Penguin Books 1964
Reprinted 1965, 1966, 1967, 1969, 1970, 1971, 1972, 1973

—

—

Made and printed in Great Britain
by Cox & Wyman Ltd,
London, Reading and Fakenham
Set in Monotype Garamond

FOR SOPHIE

*In memory of Tio Pepe, Wiener Schnitzel,
and dancing kleek to kleek*

CONTENTS

A WORD IN ADVANCE

THIS is the chronicle of a six-month trip that my wife and I
made to Bafut, a mountain grassland kingdom in the British
Cameroons in West Africa. Our reason for going there was, to
say the least, a trifle unusual. We wanted to collect our own
zoo.

Since the end of the war I had been financing and organizing
expeditions to many parts of the world to collect wild animals
for various zoological gardens. Bitter experience over the years
had taught me that the worst and most heart-breaking part of
any collecting trip came at the end when, after months of
lavishing care and attention upon them, you had to part with
the animals. If you are acting as mother, father, food-provider
and danger eradicator to an animal, half a year is enough to

build up a very real friendship with it. The creature trusts you and, what is more important, behaves naturally when you are around. Then, just when this relationship should begin to bear fruit, when you ought to be in a unique position to study the animal's habits and behaviour, you are forced to part company.

There was only one answer to this problem, as far as I was concerned, and that was to have a zoo of my own. I could then bring my animals back knowing what type of cages they were going to inhabit, what sort of food and treatment they were going to receive (a thing which one cannot, unfortunately, be sure about with some other zoos), and secure in the knowledge that I could go on studying them to my heart's content. The zoo, of course, would have to be open to the public so that, from my point of view, it would be a sort of self-supporting laboratory in which I could keep and watch my animals.

There was another and, to my mind, more urgent reason for creating a zoo. I, like many other people, have been seriously concerned by the fact that year by year, all over the world, various species of animals are being slowly but surely exterminated in their wild state, thanks directly or indirectly to the interference of mankind. While many worthy and hard-working societies are doing their best to tackle this problem, I know a great number of animal species which, because they are small and generally of no commercial or touristic value, are not receiving adequate protection. To me the extirpation of an animal species is a criminal offence, in the same way as the destruction of anything we cannot recreate or replace, such as a Rembrandt or the Acropolis. In my opinion zoological gardens all over the world should have as one of their main objects the establishment of breeding colonies for these rare and threatened species. Then, if it is inevitable that the animal should become extinct in the wild state, at least we have not lost it completely. For many years I had wanted to start a zoo with just such an object in view, and now seemed the ideal moment to begin.

Any reasonable person smitten with an ambition of this sort

would have secured the zoo first and obtained the animals after-
wards. But throughout my life I have rarely if ever achieved
what I wanted by tackling it in a logical fashion. So, naturally,
I went and got the animals first and then set about the task of
finding my zoo. This was not so easy as it might seem on the
face of it, and looking back now I am speechless at my audacity
in trying to achieve success in this way.

This, therefore, is the story of my search for a zoo, and it
explains why, for some considerable time, I had a zoo in my
luggage.

MAIL BY HAND

FROM my seat on the bougainvillaea-enshrouded verandah I looked out over the blue and glittering waters of the bay of Victoria, a bay dotted with innumerable forest-encrusted islands like little green, furry hats dropped carelessly on the surface. Two grey parrots flew swiftly across the sky, wolf-whistling to each other and calling 'coo-eee' loudly and seductively in the brilliant blue sky. A flock of tiny canoes, like a school of black fish, moved to and fro among the islands, and dimly the cries and chatter of the fishermen came drifting across the water to me. Above, in the great palms that shaded the house, a colony of weaver-birds chattered incessantly as they busily stripped the palm fronds off to weave their basket-like nests, and behind the house, where the forest began, a tinker-bird was giving its monotonous cry, toink . . . toink . . . toink . . ., like someone beating forever on a tiny anvil. The sweat was running down my spine, staining my shirt black, and the glass of beer by my side was rapidly getting warm. I was back in West Africa.

Dragging my attention away from a large, orange-headed lizard that had climbed on to the verandah rail and was busily nodding its head as if in approval of the sunshine, I turned back to my task of composing a letter.

The Fon of Bafut,
Fon's Palace,
Bafut,
Bemenda Division, British Cameroons.

I paused here for inspiration. I lit a cigarette and contemplated the sweat-marks that my fingers had left on the keys of the typewriter. I took a sip of beer and scowled at my letter. It was difficult to compose for a number of reasons.

The Fon of Bafut was a rich, clever and charming potentate who ruled over a large grassland kingdom in the mountain area of the north. Eight years previously I had spent a number of months in his country to collect the strange and rare creatures that inhabited it. The Fon had turned out to be a delightful host, and we had many fantastic parties together, for he was a great believer in enjoying life. I had marvelled at his alcoholic intake, at his immense energy and at his humour, and when I returned to England I had attempted to draw a picture of him in a book I wrote about the expedition. I had tried to show him as a shrewd and kindly man, with a great love of music, dancing, drink and other things that make life pleasant, and with an almost childlike ability for having a good time. I now wanted to revisit him in his remote and beautiful kingdom and renew our friendship; but I was a little bit worried. I had realized – too late – that the portrait I had drawn of him in my book was perhaps open to misconstruction. The Fon might well have thought that the picture was that of a senile alcoholic who spent his time getting drunk amid a bevy of wives. So it was with some trepidation that I sat down to write to him and find out if I would be welcome in his kingdom. That, I reflected, was the worst of writing books. I sighed, stubbed out my cigarette and started.

My dear friend,

As you may have heard I have returned to the Cameroons in order to catch more animals to take back to my country. As you will remember when I was last here I came up to your country and caught most of my best animals there. Also we had a very good time together.

Now I have returned with my wife and I would like her to meet you and see your beautiful country. May we come up to Bafut and stay with you while we catch our animals? I would like to stay once more in your Rest House, as I did last time, if you will let me. Perhaps you would let me know?

Yours sincerely,
Gerald Durrell

I sent this missive off by messenger together with two bottles of whisky which he was given strict instructions not to drink on the way. We then waited hopefully, day after day, while our mountain of luggage smouldered under tarpaulins in the sun, and the orange-headed lizards lay dozing on top of it. Within a week, the messenger returned and drew a letter out of the pocket of his tattered khaki shorts. I ripped open the envelope hastily and spread the letter on the table, where Jacquie and I craned over it.

Fon's Palace,
Bafut, Bemenda.
25th January 1957.

My good friend,

Yours dated 23rd received with great pleasure. I was more than pleased when I read the letter sent to me by you, in the Cameroons again.

I will be looking for you at any time you come here. How

long you think to remain with me here, no objection. My Rest House is ever ready for you at any time you arrive here.

Please pass my sincere greetings to your wife and tell her that I shall have a good chat with her when she come here.

Yours truly,
Fon of Bafut

PART ONE

EN ROUTE

MAIL BY HAND

To: The Zoological Officer.
U.A.C. Manager's House,
Mamfe.

Dearest Sir,

I have once been your customer during your first tour of the Cameroons and get you different animals.

I send here one animal with my servant, I do not know the name of it. Please could you offer what price you think fit and send it to me. The animal has been living in my house almost about three weeks and a half.

With love, sir.

I am,
Yrs sincerely,
Thomas Tambic, *Hunter*

CHAPTER ONE

THE RELUCTANT PYTHON

I HAD decided that, on the way up country to Bafut, we would make a ten-day stop at a town called Mamfe. This was at the highest navigable point of the Cross River, on the edge of an enormous tract of uninhabited country; and on the two previous occasions when I had been to the Cameroons I had found it a good collecting centre. We set off from Victoria in an impressive convoy of three lorries, Jacquie and myself in the first, our young assistant Bob in the second, and Sophie, my long-suffering secretary, in the third. The trip was hot and dusty, and we arrived at Mamfe in the brief green twilight of the third day, hungry, thirsty and covered from head to foot with a fine film of red dust. We had been told to contact the United Africa Company's manager on arrival, and so our lorries roared up the drive and screeched to a halt outside a very impressive house, ablaze with lights.

The house stood in what was certainly the best position in Mamfe. It was perched on top of a conical hill, one side of which formed part of the gorge through which the Cross River ran. From the edge of the garden, fringed with a hedge of the inevitable hibiscus bushes, you could look straight down four hundred feet into the gorge, to where a tangle of low growth and taller trees perched precariously on thirty-foot cliffs of pleated granite, thickly overgrown with wild begonias, moss and ferns. At the foot of these cliffs, round gleaming white sandbanks and strange, ribbed slabs of rock, the river wound its way like a brown, sinuous muscle. On the opposite bank there were small patches of farmland along the edge of the river, and beyond that the forest reared up in a multitude of colours and textures, spreading endlessly back until it was turned into a dim, quivering frothy green sea by distance and heat haze.

I was, however, in no mood to admire views as I uncoiled myself from the red-hot interior of the lorry and jumped to the ground. What I wanted most in the world at that moment was a drink, a bath and a meal, in that order. Almost as urgently I wanted a wooden box to house the first animal we had acquired. This was an extremely rare creature, a baby black-footed mongoose, which I had purchased from a native in a village twenty-five miles back when we had stopped there to buy some fruit. I had been delighted that we had started the collection with such a rarity, but after struggling with her for two hours in the front seat of the lorry, my enthusiasm had begun to wane. She had wanted to investigate every nook and cranny in the cab, and fearing that she might go and get tangled up in the gears and perhaps break a leg I had imprisoned her inside my shirt. For the first half-hour she had stalked round and round my body, sniffing loudly. For the next half-hour she had made several determined attempts to dig a hole in my stomach with her exceedingly sharp claws, and on being persuaded to desist from this occupation, she had seized a large portion of my abdomen in her mouth and sucked it vigorously and hopefully, while irrigating me with an apparently unending stream of warm and pungent urine. This in no way improved my already dusty and sweaty appearance, and as I marched up the steps of the U.A.C. manager's house, with a mongoose tail dangling out of my tightly buttoned, urine-stained shirt, I looked, to say the least, slightly eccentric. Taking a deep breath and trying to seem nonchalant, I walked into the brilliantly-lit living-room, and found three people seated round a card table. They looked at me with a faint air of inquiry. 'Good evening,' I said, feeling rather at a loss. 'My name's Durrell.'

It was not, I reflected, the most telling remark made in Africa since Stanley and Livingstone met. However, a small, dark man rose from the table and came towards me, smiling charmingly, his long black hair flopping down over his forehead. He held out his hand and clasped mine, and then, ignoring my sudden appearance and my unconventional condition, he peered earnestly into my face.

'Good evening,' he said. 'Do you by any chance play Canasta?'

'No,' I said, rather taken aback, 'I'm afraid I don't.'

He sighed, as if his worst fears had been realized. 'A pity ... a great pity,' he said; then he cocked his head on one side and peered at me closely.

'*What* did you say your name was?' he asked.

'Durrell ... Gerald Durrell.'

'Good hëavens,' he exclaimed, realization dawning, 'are you that animal maniac head office warned me about?'

'I expect so.'

'But my dear chap, I expected you two days ago. Where have you been?'

'We would have been here two days ago if our lorry hadn't broken down with such monotonous regularity.'

'These local lorries are bloody unreliable,' he said, as if letting me into a secret. 'Have a drink?'

'I should love one,' I said fervently. 'May I bring the others in? They're all waiting in the lorries.'

'Yes, yes, bring 'em all in. Of course. Drinks all round.'

'Thanks a lot,' I said, and turned towards the door.

My host seized me by the arm and drew me back. 'Tell me, dear boy,' he said in a hoarse whisper, 'I don't want to be personal, but is it the gin I've drunk or does your stomach *always* wriggle like that?'

'No,' I said gravely. 'It's not my stomach. I've got a mongoose in my shirt.'

He gazed at me unblinkingly for a moment.

'Very reasonable explanation,' he said at last.

'Yes,' I said, 'and true.'

He sighed. 'Well, as long as it's not the gin I don't mind *what* you keep in your shirt,' he said seriously. 'Bring the others in and we'll kill a noggin or two before you eat.'

So we invaded John Henderson's house and within a couple of days we had turned him into what must have been the most long-suffering host on the West Coast of Africa. For a man who likes his privacy to invite four strangers to live in his house is a noble deed to start with. But when he has no liking for, and a grave mistrust of, any form of animal life, to invite four animal-collectors to stay is an action so heroic that no words can describe it. Within twenty-four hours of our arrival not only a mongoose, but a squirrel, a bushbaby and two monkeys were quartered on the verandah of John's house.

While John was getting used to the idea of having his legs embraced by a half-grown baboon every time he set foot outside his own front door, I sent messages to all my old contacts among the local hunters, gathered them together and told them the sort of creatures we were after. Then we sat back and awaited results. They were some time in coming. Then, early one afternoon, a local hunter called Agustine appeared, padding down the drive, wearing a scarlet-and-blue sarong and looking, as always, like a neat, eager, Mongolian shopwalker. He was accompanied by one of the largest West Africans I have ever seen, a great, scowling man who must have been at least six feet tall, and whose skin – in contrast to Agustine's golden bronze shade – was a deep soot black. He clumped along beside Agustine on such enormous feet that at first I thought he was suffering from elephantiasis. They stopped at the verandah steps, and while Agustine beamed cheerily, his companion glared at us in a preoccupied manner, as though endeavouring to assess our net weight for culinary purposes.

'Good morning, sah,' said Agustine, giving a twist to his highly-coloured sarong to anchor it more firmly round his slim hips.

'Good morning, sah,' intoned the giant, his voice sounding like the distant rumble of thunder.

'Good morning . . . you bring beef?' I inquired hopefully, though they did not appear to be carrying any animals.

'No, sah,' said Agustine sorrowfully, 'we no get beef. I come to ask Masa if Masa go borrow us some rope.'

'Rope? What do you want rope for?'

'We done find some big boa, sah, for bush. But we no fit catch um if we no get rope, sah.'

Bob, whose speciality was reptiles, sat up with a jerk.

'Boa?' he said excitedly. 'What does he mean . . . boa?'

'They mean a python,' I explained. One of the most confusing things about pidgin English, from the naturalist's point of view, was the number of wrong names used for various animals. Pythons were boas, leopards were tigers and so on. Bob's eyes gleamed with a fanatical light. Ever since we had boarded the ship at Southampton his conversation had been almost entirely confined to pythons, and I knew that he would not be really happy until he had added one of these reptiles to the collection.

'Where is it?' he asked, his voice quivering with ill-concealed eagerness.

''E dere dere for bush,' said Agustine, waving a vague arm that embraced approximately five hundred square miles of forest. ''E dere dere for some hole inside ground.'

'Na big one?' I asked.

'Wah! Big?' exclaimed Agustine. ''E big too much.'

''E big like dis,' said the giant, slapping his thigh which was about the size of a side of beef.

'We walka for bush since morning time, sah,' explained Agustine. 'Den we see dis boa. We run quick-quick, but we no catch lucky. Dat snake get power too much. 'E done run for some hole for ground and we no get rope so we no fit catch um.'

'You done leave some man for watch dis hole,' I asked, 'so dis boa no go run for bush?'

'Yes, sah, we done lef' two men for dere.'

I turned to Bob. 'Well, here's your chance: a genuine wild python holed up in a cave. Shall we go and have a shot at it?'

'God, yes! Let's go and get it right away,' exclaimed Bob.

I turned to Agustine. 'We go come look dis snake, Agustine, eh?'

'Yes, sah.'

'You go wait small time and we go come. First we get rope and catch net.'

While Bob hurried out to our pile of equipment to fetch rope and nets, I filled a couple of bottles with water and rounded up Ben, our animal boy, who was squatting outside the back door, flirting with a damsel of voluptuous charms.

'Ben, leave that unfortunate young woman alone and get ready. We're going for bush to catch a boa.'

'Yes, sah,' said Ben, reluctantly leaving his girl friend. 'Which side dis boa, sah?'

'Agustine say it's in a hole for ground. That's why I want you. If this hole is so small that Mr Golding and I no fit pass you will have to go for inside and catch the boa.'

'Me, sah?' said Ben.

'Yes, you. All alone.'

'All right,' he said, grinning philosophically. 'I no de fear, sah.'

'You lie,' I said. 'You know you de fear too much.'

'I no de fear, for true, sah,' said Ben in a dignified manner. 'I never tell Masa how I done kill bush-cow?'

'Yes, you told me twice, and I still don't believe you. Now, go to Mr Golding and get the ropes and catch nets. Hurry.'

To reach the area of country in which our quarry was waiting, we had to go down the hill and cross the river by the ferry, a large, banana-shaped canoe which appeared to have been constructed about three centuries ago, and to have been deteriorating slowly ever since. It was paddled by a very old man who looked in immediate danger of dying of a heart attack, and he was accompanied by a small boy whose job it was to bale out. This was something of an unequal struggle, for the boy had a small rusty tin for the job, while the sides of the canoe were as watertight as a colander. Inevitably, by the time one reached the opposite bank one was sitting in about six inches of water. When we arrived with our equipment on the water-worn steps in the granite cliff that formed the landing-stage, we found the ferry was at the opposite shore, so while Ben, Agustine and the enormous African (whom we had christened Gargantua) lifted their voices and roared at the ferryman to return with all speed, Bob and I squatted in the shade and watched the usual crowd of Mamfe people bathing and washing in the brown waters below.

Swarms of small boys leapt shrieking off the cliffs and splashed into the water, and then shot to the surface again, their palms and the soles of their feet gleaming shell pink, their bodies like polished chocolate. The girls, more demure, bathed in their sarongs, only to emerge from the water with the cloth clinging to their bodies so tightly that it left nothing to the imagination. One small toddler, who could not have been more than five or six, made his way carefully down the cliff, his tongue protruding with concentration, carrying on his head an enormous water-jar. On reaching the edge of the water he did not pause to remove the jar from his head, or to take off his sarong. He walked straight into the water and waded slowly and determinedly out into the river until he completely disappeared; only the jar could be seen moving mysteriously along the surface of the water. At length this too vanished. There was a moment's pause, and then the jar reappeared, this time moving shorewards, and eventually, beneath it, the boy's head bobbed up. He gave a tremendous snort to expel the air from his lungs, and then struggled grimly towards the beach, the now brimming jar on his head. When he reached the shore he edged the jar carefully on to a ledge of rock, and then re-entered the water, still wearing his sarong. From some intricate fold in his garment he produced a small fragment of Lifebuoy soap, and proceeded to rub it all over himself and the sarong with complete impartiality. Presently, when he had worked up such a lather all over himself that he looked like an animated pink snowman, he ducked beneath the surface to wash off the soap, waded ashore, settled the jar once more on his head and slowly climbed the cliff and disappeared. It was the perfect example of the African application of time-and-motion study.

By this time the ferry had arrived, and Ben and Agustine were arguing hotly with its aged occupant. Instead of taking us straight across the river, they wanted him to paddle us about half a mile upstream to a large sandbank. This would save us having to walk about a mile along the bank to reach the path that led to the forest. The old man appeared to be singularly obstinate about the proposal.

'What's the matter with him, Ben?' I inquired.

'Eh! Dis na foolish man, sah,' said Ben, turning to me in exasperation, ''e no agree for take us for up de river.'

'Why you no agree, my friend?' I asked the old man. 'If you go take us I go pay you more money and I go dash you.'

'Masa,' said the old man firmly, 'dis na my boat, and if I go lose um I no fit catch money again . . . I no get chop for my belly . . . I no get one-one penny.'

'But how you go lose you boat?' I asked in amazement, for I knew this strip of river and there were no rapids or bad currents along it.

'Ipopo, Masa,' explained the old man.

I stared at the ferryman, wondering what on earth he was talking about. Was Ipopo perhaps some powerful local juju I had not come across before?

'Dis Ipopo,' I asked soothingly, 'which side 'e live?'

'Wah! Masa never see um?' asked the old man in astonishment. ''E dere dere for water close to D.O.'s house . . . 'e big like so-so motor . . . 'e de holla . . . 'e de get power too much.'

'What's he talking about?' asked Bob in bewilderment.

And suddenly it dawned on me. 'He's talking about the hippo herd in the river below the D.O.'s house,' I explained, 'but it's such a novel abbreviation of the word that he had me foxed for a moment.'

'Does he think they're dangerous?'

'Apparently, though I can't think why. They were perfectly placid last time I was here.'

'Well, I hope they're still placid,' said Bob.

I turned to the old man again. 'Listen, my friend. If you go take us for up dis water, I go pay you six shilling and I go dash you cigarette, eh? And if sometime dis ipopo go damage dis your boat I go pay for new one, you hear?'

'I hear, sah.'

'You agree?'

'I agree, sah,' said the old man, avarice struggling with caution. We progressed slowly upstream, squatting in half an inch of water in the belly of the canoe.

'I suppose they can't really be dangerous,' said Bob casually, trailing his hand nonchalantly in the water.

'When I was here last I used to go up to within thirty feet of them in a canoe and take photographs,' I said.

'Dis ipopo get strong head now, sah,' said Ben tactlessly. 'Two months pass dey kill three men and break two boats.'

'That's a comforting thought,' said Bob.

Ahead of us the brown waters were broken in many places by rocks. At any other time they would have looked exactly like rocks but now each one looked exactly like the head of a hippo, a cunning, maniacal hippo, lurking in the dark waters, awaiting our approach. Ben, presumably remembering his tale of daring with the bush-cow, attempted to whistle, but it was a feeble effort, and I noticed that he scanned the waters ahead anxiously. After all, a hippo that has developed the habit of attacking canoes gets a taste for it, like a man-eating tiger, and will go out of his way to be unpleasant, apparently regarding it as a sport. I was not feeling in the mood for gambolling in twenty feet of murky water with half a ton of sadistic hippo.

The old man, I noticed, was keeping our craft well into the bank, twisting and turning so that we were, as far as possible, always in shallow water. The cliff here was steep, but well supplied with footholds in case of emergency, for the rocks lay folded in great layers like untidy piles of fossilized magazines, overgrown with greenery. The trees that grew on top of the cliffs spread their branches well out over the water, so that we travelled in a series of fish-like jerks up a tunnel of shade, startling the occasional kingfisher that whizzed across our bows like a vivid blue shooting-star, or a black-and-white wattled plover that flapped away upstream, tittering imbecilically to itself, with its feet grazing the water, and long yellow wattles flapping absurdly on each side of its beak.

Gradually we rounded the bend of the river, and there, about three hundred yards ahead of us on the opposite shore, lay the white bulk of the sandbank, frilled with ripples. The old man gave a grunt of relief at the sight, and started to paddle more swiftly.

'Nearly there,' I said gaily, 'and not a hippo in sight.'

The words were hardly out of my mouth when a rock we were passing some fifteen feet away suddenly rose out of the water and gazed at us with bulbous astonished eyes, snorting out two slender fountains of spray, like a miniature whale.

Fortunately, our gallant crew resisted the impulse to leap out of the canoe *en masse* and swim for the bank. The old man drew in his breath with a sharp hiss, and dug his paddle deep into the water, so that the canoe pulled up short in a swirl and clop of bubbles. Then we sat and stared at the hippo, and the hippo sat and stared at us. Of the two, the hippo seemed the more astonished. The chubby, pink-grey face floated on the surface of the water like a disembodied head at a séance. The great eyes stared at us with the innocent appraisal of a baby. The ears flicked back and forth, as if waving to us. The hippo sighed deeply and moved a few feet nearer, still looking at us with wide-eyed innocence. Then, suddenly, Agustine let out a shrill whoop that made us all jump and nearly upset the canoe. We shushed him furiously, while the hippo continued its scrutiny of us unabashed.

'No de fear,' said Agustine in a loud voice, 'na woman.'

He seized the paddle from the old man's reluctant grasp, and proceeded to beat on the water with the blade, sending up a shower of spray. The hippo opened its mouth in a gigantic yawn to display a length of tooth that had to be seen to be believed. Then, suddenly, and with apparently no muscular effort, the great head sank beneath the surface. There was a moment's pause, during which we were all convinced that the beast was ploughing through the water somewhere directly beneath us, then the head rose to the surface again, this time, to our relief, about twenty yards up-river. It snorted out two more jets of spray, waggled its ears seductively and sank again, only to reappear in a moment or so still farther upstream. The old man grunted and retrieved his paddle from Agustine.

'Agustine, why you do dat foolish ting?' I asked in what I hoped was a steady and trenchant tone of voice.

'Sah, dat ipopo no be man . . . na woman dat,' Agustine explained, hurt by my lack of faith in him.

'How you know?' I demanded.

'Masa, I savvay all dis ipopo for dis water,' he explained, 'dis one na woman. Ef na man ipopo 'e go chop us one time. But dis woman one no get strong head like 'e husband.'

'Well, thank God for the weaker sex,' I said to Bob, as the old man, galvanized into activity, sent the canoe shooting diagonally across the river, so that it ground on to the sandbank in a shower of pebbles. We unloaded our gear, told the old man to wait for us and set off towards the python's lair.

The path lay at first through some old native farmland, where the giant trees had been felled and now lay rotting across the ground. Between these trunks a crop of cassava had been grown and harvested, and the ground allowed to lie fallow, so that the low growth of the forest – thorn bushes, convolvulus and other tangles – had swept into the clearing and covered everything with a cloak. There was always plenty of life to be seen in these abandoned farms, and as we pushed through the intricate web of undergrowth there were birds all around us. Beautiful little flycatchers hovered in the air, showing up powder-blue against the greenery; in the dim recesses of convolvulus-covered tree stumps robin-chats hopped perkily in search of grasshoppers, and looked startlingly like English robins; a pied crow flew up from the ground ahead and flapped heavily away, crying a harsh warning; in a thicket of thorn bushes, covered with pink flowers among which zoomed big blue bees, a kurrichane thrush treated us to a waterfall of sweet song. The path wound its way through this moist, hot, waist-high undergrowth for some time, and then quite abruptly the undergrowth ended and the path led us out on to a golden grassfield, rippling with the heat haze.

Attractive though they were to look at, these grassfields were far from comfortable to walk across. The grass was tough and spiky, growing in tussocks carefully placed to trip the unwary traveller. In places, where sheets of grey rocks were exposed to the sun, the surface, sprinkled with a million tiny mica chips, sparkled and flashed in your eyes. The sun beat down upon your neck, and its reflections rebounded off the glittering surface of the rock and hit you in the face with the impact of a blast furnace. We plodded across this sun-drenched expanse, the sweat pouring off us.

'I hope this damned reptile's had the sense to go to ground where there's some shade,' I said to Bob. 'You could fry an egg on these rocks.'

Agustine, who had been padding eagerly ahead, his sarong turning from scarlet to wine-red as it absorbed the sweat from his body, turned and grinned at me, his face freckled with a mass of sweat-drops.

'Masa hot?' he inquired anxiously.

'Yes, hot too much,' I answered, ''e far now dis place?'

'No, sah,' he said pointing ahead, ''e dere dere. . . . Masa never see dis man I done leave for watch?'

I followed his pointing finger and in the distance I could see an area where the rocks had been pushed up and rumpled, like bedclothes, by some ancient volcanic upheaval, so that they formed a miniature cliff running diagonally across the grass-field. On top of this I could see the figures of two more hunters, squatting patiently in the sun. When they saw us they rose to their feet and waved ferocious-looking spears in greeting.

''E dere dere for hole?' yelled Agustine anxiously.

''E dere dere,' they called back.

When we reached the base of the small cliff I could quite see why the python had chosen this spot to stand at bay. The rock face had been split into a series of shallow caves, worn smooth by wind and water, each communicating with the other, and the whole series sloping slightly upwards into the cliff, so that anything that lived in them would be in no danger of getting drowned in the rainy season. The mouth of each cave was about eight feet across and three feet high, which gave a snake, but not much else, room for manoeuvring. The hunters had very thoughtfully set fire to all the grass in the vicinity, in an effort to smoke the reptile out. The snake had been unaffected by this, but now we had to work in a thick layer of charcoal and feathery ash up to our ankles.

Bob and I got down on our stomachs and, shoulder to shoulder, wormed our way into the mouth of the cave to try and spot the python and map out a plan of campaign. We soon found that the cave narrowed within three or four feet of the entrance so that there was only room for one person, lying as flat as he could. After the glare of the sunshine outside, the cave seemed twice as dark as it was, and we could not see a thing. The only indication that a snake was there at all was a loud peevish hissing every time we moved. We called loudly for a torch, and when this had been unpacked and handed to us we directed its beam up the narrow passage.

Eight feet ahead of us the passage ended in a circular depression in the rock, and in this the python lay coiled, shining in the torchlight as if freshly polished. It was about fifteen feet long as far as we could judge, and so fat that we pardoned Gargantua for comparing its girth with his enormous thigh. It was also in an extremely bad temper. The longer the torch beam played on it the more prolonged and shrill did its hisses become, until they rose to an eerie shriek. We crawled out into the sunlight again and sat up, both of us almost the same colour as our hunters because of the thick layer of dark ash adhering to our sweaty bodies.

'The thing is to get a noose round its neck, and then we can all pull like hell and drag it out,' said Bob.

'Yes, but the job's going to be to *get* the noose round its neck. I don't fancy being wedged in that passage if it decided to come down it after one. There's no room to manoeuvre, and there's no room for anyone to help you if you do get entangled with it.'

'Yes, that's a point,' Bob admitted.

'There's only one thing to do,' I said. 'Agustine, go quick-quick and cut one fork-stick for me . . . big one . . . you hear?'

'Yes, sah,' said Agustine, and whipping out his broad-bladed machete he trotted off towards the forest's edge some three hundred yards away.

'Remember,' I warned Bob, 'if we *do* succeed in yanking it out into the open, you can't rely on the hunters. Everyone in the Cameroons is convinced that a python is poisonous; not only do they think its bite is deadly, but they also think it can poison you with the spurs under the tail. So if we do get it out its no good grabbing the head and expecting them to hang on to the tail. You'll have to grab one end while I grab the other, and we'll just have to hope to heaven that they co-operate in the middle.

'That's a jolly thought,' said Bob, sucking his teeth meditatively.

Presently Agustine returned, carrying a long, straight sapling with a fork at one end. On to this forked end I fastened a slip knot with some fine cord which, the manufacturers had assured me, would stand a strain of three hundredweight. Then I unravelled fifty feet or so of the cord, and handed the rest of the coil to Agustine.

'Now I go for inside, I go try put dis rope for 'e neck, eh? If I go catch 'e neck I go holla, and then all dis hunter man go pull one time. You hear?'

'I hear, sah.'

'Now if I should pull,' I said, as I lowered myself delicately into the carpet of ash, 'for Heaven's sake don't let them pull too hard. . . . I don't want the damn thing pulled on top of me.'

I wriggled slowly up the cave, carrying the sapling and cord with me, the torch in my mouth. The python hissed with undiminished ferocity. Then came the delicate job of trying to push the sapling ahead of me so that I could get the dangling noose over the snake's head. I found this impossible with the torch in my mouth, for at the slightest movement the beam swept everywhere but on to the point required. I put the torch on the ground, propped it up on some rocks with the beam playing on the snake and then, with infinite care, I edged the sapling up the cave towards the reptile. The python had, of course, coiled itself into a tight knot, with the head lying in the centre of coils, so when I had got the sapling into position I had to force the snake to show its head. The only way of doing this was to prod the creature vigorously with the end of the sapling.

After the first prod the shining coils seemed to swell with rage, and there came echoing down the cave a hiss so shrill and so charged with malignancy that I almost dropped the sapling. Grasping the wood more firmly in my sweaty hand I prodded again, and was treated to another shrill exhalation of breath. Five times I prodded before my efforts were rewarded. The python's head appeared suddenly over the top of the coils, and swept towards the end of the sapling, the mouth wide open and gleaming pinkly in the torchlight. But the movement was so sudden that I had no chance to get the noose over its head. The snake struck three times, and each time I made ineffectual attempts to noose it. My chief difficulty was that I could not get close enough; I was working at the full stretch of my arm, and this, combined with the weight of the sapling, made my movements very clumsy. At last, dripping with sweat, my arms aching, I crawled out into the sunlight.

'It's no good,' I said to Bob. 'It keeps its head buried in its coils and only pops it out to strike ... you don't get a real chance to noose it.'

'Let me have a go,' he said eagerly.

He seized the sapling and crawled into the cave. There was a long pause during which we could only see his large feet scrabbling and scraping for a foothold in the cave entrance. Presently he reappeared, cursing fluently.

'It's no good,' he said. 'We'll never get it with this.'

'If they get us a forked stick like a shepherd's crook do you think you could get hold of a coil and pull it out?' I inquired.

'I think so,' said Bob, 'or at any rate I could probably make it uncoil so we can get a chance at the head.'

So Agustine was once more dispatched to the forest with minute instructions as to the sort of stick we needed, and he soon returned with a twenty-foot branch at one end of which was a fish-hook-like projection.

'If you could crawl in with me and shine the torch over my shoulder, it would help,' said Bob. 'If I put it on the ground, I knock it over every time I move.'

So we crawled into the cave together and lay there, wedged

shoulder to shoulder. While I shone the torch down the tunnel, Bob slowly edged his gigantic crook towards the snake. Slowly, so as not to disturb the snake unnecessarily, he edged the hook over the top coil of the mound, settled it in place, shuffled his body into a more comfortable position and then hauled with all his strength.

The results were immediate and confusing. To our surprise the entire bulk of the snake – after a momentary resistance – slid down the cave towards us. Exhilarated, Bob shuffled backwards (thus wedging us both more tightly in the tunnel) and hauled again. The snake slid still nearer and then started to unravel. Bob hauled again, and the snake uncoiled still farther; its head and neck appeared out of the tangle and struck at us. Wedged like a couple of outsize sardines in an undersized can we had no room to move except backwards, and so we slid backwards on our stomachs as rapidly as we could. At last, to our relief, we reached a slight widening in the passage, and this allowed us more room to manoeuvre. Bob laid hold of the sapling and pulled at it grimly. He reminded me of a lanky and earnest blackbird tugging an outsize worm from its hole. The snake slid into view, hissing madly, its coils shuddering with muscular contraction as it tried to free itself of the hook round its body. Another good heave, I calculated, and Bob would have it at the mouth of the cave. I crawled out rapidly.

'Bring dat rope,' I roared to the hunters, 'quick . . . quick . . . rope.'

They leapt to obey as Bob appeared at the cave mouth, scrambled to his feet and stepped back for the final jerk that would drag the snake out into the open where we could fall on it. But, as he stepped back, he put his foot on a loose rock which twisted under him, and he fell flat on his back. The sapling was jerked from his hands, the snake gave a mighty heave that freed its body from the hook, and, with the smooth fluidity of water soaking into blotting-paper it slid into a crack in the cave wall that did not look as though it could accommodate a mouse. As the last four feet of its length were disappearing into the bowels of the earth, Bob and I fell on it and hung on like grim death. We could feel the rippling of the powerful muscles as the snake, buried deep in the rocky cleft, struggled to break our grip on its tail. Slowly, inch by inch, the smooth scales slipped through our sweaty hands, and then, suddenly, the snake was gone. From somewhere deep in the rocks came a triumphant hiss.

Covered with ash and charcoal smears, our arms and legs scraped raw, our clothes black with sweat, Bob and I sat and glared at each other, panting for breath. We were past speech.

'Ah, 'e done run, Masa,' pointed out Agustine, who seemed to have a genius for underlining the obvious.

'Dat snake 'e get power too much,' observed Gargantua moodily.

'No man fit hold dat snake for inside hole,' said Agustine, attempting to comfort us.

''E get plenty, plenty power,' intoned Gargantua again, ''e get power pass man.'

In silence I handed round the cigarettes and we squatted in the carpet of ash and smoked.

'Well,' I said at last, philosophically, 'we did the best we could. Let's hope for better luck next time.'

Bob, however, refused to be comforted. To have had the python of his dreams so close to capture and then to lose it was almost more than he could bear. He prowled around, muttering savagely to himself, as we packed up the nets and ropes, and then followed us moodily as we set off homewards.

The sun was now low in the sky, and by the time we had crossed the grassfield and entered the abandoned farmland a greenish twilight had settled on the world. Everywhere in the moist undergrowth giant glow-worms gleamed and shuddered like sapphires, and through the warm air fireflies drifted, pulsating briefly like pink pearls against the dark undergrowth. The air was full of the evening scents, wood smoke, damp earth, the sweet smell of blossom already wet with dew. An owl called in an ancient, trembling voice, and another answered it.

The river was like a moving sheet of bronze in the twilight as we scrunched our way across the milk-white sandbank. The old man and the boy were curled up alseep in the bows of the canoe. They awoke, and in silence paddled us down the dark river. On the hill top, high above us, we could see the lamps of the house shining out, and faintly, as a background to the swish and gurgle of our paddles, we could hear the gramophone playing. A drift of small white moths enveloped the canoe as it headed towards the bank. The moon, very fragile and weak, was edging its way up through the filigree of the forest behind us, and once more the owls called, sadly, longingly, in the gloom of the trees.

To: Mr G. Durrell,
The Zoological Department,
U.A.C. House,
Mamfe.

Dear Sir,
Here are two animals I am senting you like those animals that
you should me in the pictures. Any tipe of money you want to
sent to me try and rapp the money in a small piece of paper
and sent it to that boy that brought animals. You know realy
that a hunter always be derty so you should try to send me one
bar soap.
Good greetings to you.

Yrs,
Peter N'amabong

CHAPTER TWO

THE BALD-HEADED BIRDS

On the opposite bank of the Cross River, eight miles through the deep forest, lay the tiny village of Eshobi. I knew both the place and its inhabitants well, for on a previous trip I had made it one of my bases for a number of months. It had been a good hunting-ground, and the Eshobi people had been good hunters, so, while we were in Mamfe, I was anxious to get in touch with the villagers and see if they could get us some specimens. As the best way of obtaining information or sending messages was via the local market, I sent for Phillip, our cook. He was an engaging character, with a wide, buck-toothed smile, and a habit of walking with a stiff military gait, and standing at attention when addressed; this argued an army training, which, in fact, he had not had. He clumped up on to the verandah and stood before me as rigid as a guardsman.

'Phillip, I want to find an Eshobi man, you hear?' I said.

'Yes, sah.'

'Now, when you go for market you go find me one Eshobi man and you go bring him for here and I go give him book for take Eshobi, eh?'

'Yes, sah.'

'Now, you no go forget, eh? You go find me Eshobi man one time.'

'Yes, sah,' said Phillip, and clumped off to the kitchen. He never wasted time on unnecessary conversation.

Two days passed without an Eshobi man putting in an appearance, and, occupied with other things, I forgot the whole matter. Then, on the fourth day, Phillip appeared, clumping down the drive triumphantly with a rather frightened looking fourteen-year-old boy in tow. The lad had obviously clad himself in his best clothes for his visit to the Metropolis of Mamfe, a fetching outfit that consisted of a tattered pair of khaki shorts, and a grubby white shirt which had obviously been made out of a sack of some sort and had across its back the mysterious but decorative message 'PRODUCE OF GR' in blue lettering. On his head was perched a straw hat which, with age and wear, had attained a pleasant shade of pale silvery green. This reluctant apparition was dragged up on to the front verandah, and his captor stood smugly to attention with the air of one who has, after much practice, accomplished a particularly difficult conjuring trick. Phillip had a curious way of speaking which had taken me some time to understand, for he spoke pidgin very fast and in a sort of muted roar, a cross between a bassoon and a regimental sergeant-major, as though everyone in the world was deaf. When labouring under excitement he became almost incomprehensible.

'Who is this?' I asked, surveying the youth.

Phillip looked rather hurt. 'Dis na man, sah,' he roared, as if explaining something to a particularly dim-witted child. He gazed at his protégé with affection and gave the unfortunate lad a slap on the back that almost knocked him off the verandah.

'I can see it's a man,' I said patiently, 'but what does he want?'

Phillip frowned ferociously at the quivering youth and gave him another blow between the shoulder blades.

'Speak now,' he blared, 'speak now, Masa de wait.'

We waited expectantly. The youth shuffled his feet, twiddled his toes in an excess of embarrassment, gave a shy, watery smile and stared at the ground. We waited patiently. Suddenly he looked up, removed his headgear, ducked his head and said: 'Good morning, sah,' in a faint voice.

Phillip beamed at me as if this greeting were sufficient explanation for the lad's presence. Deciding that my cook had not been designed by nature to play the part of a skilled and tactful interrogator, I took over myself.

'My friend,' I said, 'how dey de call you?'

'Peter, sah,' he replied miserably.

'Dey de call um Peter, sah,' bellowed Phillip, in case I should have been under any misapprehension.

'Well, Peter, why you come for see me?' I inquired.

'Masa, dis man your cook 'e tell me Masa want some man for carry book to Eshobi,' said the youth aggrievedly.

'Ah! You be Eshobi man?' I asked, light dawning.

'Yes, sah.'

'Phillip,' I said, 'you are a congenital idiot.'

'Yes, sah,' agreed Phillip, pleased with this unsolicited testimonial.

'Why you never tell me dis be Eshobi man?'

'Wah!' gasped Phillip, shocked to the depths of his sergeant-major's soul, 'but I done tell Masa dis be man.'

Giving Phillip up as a bad job I turned back to the youth.

'Listen, my friend, you savvay for Eshobi one man dey de call Elias?'

'Yes, sah, I savvay um.'

'All right. Now you go tell Elias dat I done come for Cameroon again for catch beef, eh? You go tell um I want um work hunter man again for me, eh? So you go tell um he go come for Mamfe for talk with me. You go tell um, say, dis Masa 'e live for U.A.C. Masa's house, you hear?'

'I hear, sah.'

'Right, so you go walk quick-quick to Eshobi and tell Elias, eh? I go dash you dis cigarette so you get happy when you walk for bush.'

He received the packet of cigarettes in his cupped hands, ducked his head and beamed at me.

'Tank you, Masa,' he said.

'All right . . . go for Eshobi now. Walka good.'

'Tank you, Masa,' he repeated, and stuffing the packet into the pocket of his unorthodox shirt he trotted off down the drive.

Twenty-four hours later Elias arrived. He had been one of my permanent hunters when I had been in Eshobi, so I was delighted to see his fat, waddling form coming down the drive towards me, his Pithecanthropic features split into a wide grin of glad recognition. Our greetings over, he solemnly handed me a dozen eggs carefully wrapped in banana leaves, and I reciprocated with a carton of cigarettes and a hunting knife I had brought out from England for that purpose. Then we got down to the serious business of talking about beef. First he told me about all the beef he had hunted and captured in my eight years' absence, and how my various hunter friends had got on. Old N'ago had been killed by a bush-cow; Andraia had been bitten in the foot by a water beef; Samuel's gun had exploded and blown a large portion of his arm away (a good joke, this), while just recently John had killed the biggest bush-pig they had ever seen, and sold the meat for over two pounds. Then, quite suddenly, Elias said something that riveted my attention.

'Masa remember dat bird Masa like too much?' he inquired in his husky voice.

'Which bird, Elias?'

'Dat bird 'e no get bere-bere for 'e head. Last time Masa live· for Mamfe I done bring um two picken dis bird.'

'Dat bird who make his house with potta-potta? Dat one who get red for his head?' I asked excitedly.

'Yes, na dis one,' he agreed.

'Well, what about it?' I said.

'When I hear Masa done come back for Cameroons I done go for bush for look dis bird,' Elias explained. 'I remember dat Masa 'e like dis bird *too much*. I look um, look um for bush for two, three days.'

He paused and looked at me, his eyes twinkling.

'Well?'

'I done find um, Masa,' he said, grinning from ear to ear.

'You find um?' I could scarcely believe my luck. 'Which side 'e dere ... which side 'e live ... how many you see ... what kind of place ...?'

''E dere dere,' Elias went on, interrupting my flow of feverish questions, 'for some place 'e get big big rock. 'E live for up hill, sah. 'E get 'e house for some big rock.'

'How many house you see?'

'I see three, sah. But 'e never finish one house, sah.'

'What's all the excitement about?' inquired Jacquie, who had just come out on to the verandah.

'*Picathartes*,' I said succinctly, and to her credit she knew exactly what I was talking about.

Picathartes was a bird that, until a few years ago, was known only from a few museum skins, and had been observed in the wild state by perhaps two Europeans. Cecil Webb, then the London Zoo's official collector, managed to catch and bring back alive the first specimen of this extraordinary bird. Six months later, when in the Cameroons, I had two adult specimens brought in to me, but these had unfortunately died on the voyage home of aspergillosis, a particularly virulent lung disease. Now Elias had found a nesting colony of them and it

seemed we might, with luck, be able to get some fledglings and
hand-rear them.

'Dis bird, 'e get picken for inside 'e house?' I asked Elias.

'Sometime 'e get, sah,' he said doubtfully. 'I never look for
inside de house. I fear sometime de bird go run.'

'Well,' I said, turning to Jacquie, 'there's only one thing to
do, and that's to go to Eshobi and have a look. You and Sophie
hang on here and look after the collection; I'll take Bob and
spend a couple of days there after *Picathartes*. Even if they
haven't got any young I would like to see the thing in its wild
state.'

'All right. When will you go?' asked Jacquie.

'Tomorrow, if I can arrange carriers. Give Bob a shout and
tell him we're really going into the forest at last. Tell him to
sort out his snake-catching equipment.'

Early the next morning, when the air was still comparatively
cool, eight Africans appeared outside John Henderson's
house, and, after the usual bickering as to who should carry
what, they loaded our bundles of equipment on to their woolly
heads and we set off for Eshobi. Having crossed the river, our
little cavalcade made its way across the grassfield, where our
abortive python hunt occurred, and on the opposite side we
plunged into the mysterious forest. The Eshobi path lay twisting and turning through the trees in a series of intricate con-
volutions that would have horrified a Roman road-builder.
Sometimes it doubled back on itself to avoid a huge rock,
or a fallen tree, and at other times it ran as straight as a rod
through all such obstacles, so that our carriers were forced to
stop and form a human chain to lift the loads over a tree trunk,
or lower them down a small cliff.

I had warned Bob that we would see little, if any, wild life
on the way, but this did not prevent him from attacking every
rotten tree trunk we passed, in the hopes of unearthing some
rare beast from inside it. I am so tired of hearing and reading
about the dangerous and evil tropical forest, teeming with wild

beasts. In the first place it is about as dangerous as the New Forest in midsummer, and in the second place it does not teem with wild life; every bush is *not* aquiver with some savage creature waiting to pounce. The animals are there, of course, but they very sensibly keep out of your way. I defy anyone to walk through the forest to Eshobi, and, at the end of it, be able to count on the fingers of both hands the 'wild beasts' he has seen. How I wish these descriptions were true. How I wish that every bush did contain some 'savage denizen of the forest' lurking in ambush. A collector's job would be so much easier.

The only wild creatures at all common along the Eshobi path were butterflies, and these, obviously not having read the right books, showed a strong disinclination to attack us. Whenever the path dipped into a small valley, a tiny stream would lie at the bottom, and on the damp, shady banks alongside the clear waters the butterflies would be sitting in groups, their wings opening and closing slowly, so that from a distance areas of the stream banks took on an opalescent quality, changing from flame red to white, from sky blue to mauve and purple, as the insects – in a sort of trance – seemed to be applauding the cool shade with their wings. The brown, muscular legs of the carriers would tramp through them unseeingly, and suddenly we would be waist-high in a swirling merry-go-round of colour as the butterflies dipped and wheeled around us and then, when we had passed, settled again on the dark soil which was as rich and moist as a fruit cake, and just as fragrant.

One vast and ancient tree marked the half-way point on the Eshobi road, a tree so tangled in a web of lianas as to be almost invisible. This was a resting place, and the carriers, grunting and exhaling their breath sharply through their front teeth in a sort of exhausted whistle, lowered their loads to the ground and squatted beside them, the sweat glistening on their bodies. I handed round cigarettes and we sat and enjoyed them quietly: in the dim, cathedral-like gloom of the forest there was no breeze, and the smoke rose in straight, swaying blue columns into the air. The only sounds were the incessant, circular-saw songs of the great green cicadas clinging to every tree, and, in the distance, the drunken honking of a flock of hornbills.

As we smoked we watched some of the little brown forest skinks hunting among the roots of the trees around us. These little lizards always looked neat and shining, as though they had been cast in chocolate and had just that second stepped out of the mould, gleaming and immaculate. They moved slowly and deliberately, as if they were afraid of getting their beautiful skins dirty. They peered from side to side with bright eyes as they slid through their world of brown, dead leaves, forests of tiny toadstools and lawns of moss that padded the stones like a carpet. Their prey was the immense population of tiny creatures that inhabited the forest floor, the small black beetles hurrying along like undertakers late for a funeral, the slow, smooth-sliding slugs, weaving a silver filigree of slime over the leaves, and the small, nut-brown crickets who squatted in the shadows waving their immensely long antennae to and fro, like amateur fishermen on the banks of a stream.

Among the dark, damp hollows between the buttress roots of the great tree under which we sat there were small clusters of an insect which had never failed to fascinate me. They looked like a small daddy-longlegs in repose, but with opaque, misty-white wings. They sat there in groups of about ten, trembling their wings gently, and moving their fragile legs up and down like restive horses. When disturbed they all took to the air and started a combined operation which was quite extraordinary to watch. They rose about eight inches above the ground, formed a circle in an area that could be covered by a saucer and then began to fly round and round very rapidly, some going up and over, as it were, while the others swept round and round like a wheel. The effect from a distance was rather weird, for they resembled a whirling ball of shimmering misty white, changing its shape slightly at intervals, but always maintaining exactly the same position in the air. They flew so fast, and their bodies were so slender, that all you could see was this shimmer of frosty wings. I am afraid that this aerial display intrigued me so much that I used to go out of my way, when walking in the forest, to find groups of these insects and disturb them so that they would dance for me.

Eventually we reached Eshobi at mid-day, and I found it had changed little from the days when I had been there eight years before. There was still the same straggle of dusty thatched huts in two uneven rows, with a wide area of dusty path lying between them that served as the village high street, a playground for children and dogs and a scratching ground for the scrawny fowls. Elias came waddling down this path to greet us, picking his way carefully through the sprawling mass of babies and livestock, followed by a small boy carrying two large green coconuts on his head.

'Welcome, Masa, you done come?' he called huskily.

'Iseeya, Elias,' I replied.

He grinned at us delightedly, as the carriers, still grunting and whistling, deposited our equipment all over the village street.

'Masa go drink dis coconut?' Elias asked hopefully, waving his machete about.

'Yes, we like um too much,' I said, regarding the huge nuts thirstily.

Elias bustled into activity. From the nearest hut were brought two dilapidated chairs, and Bob and I were seated in a small patch of shade in the centre of the village street, surrounded by a crowd of politely silent but deeply fascinated Eshobites. With quick, accurate strokes of his machete Elias stripped away the thick husk from the coconut. When the tips of the nuts were exposed he gave each of them a swift slice with the end of his machete-blade, and then handed them to us, each neatly trepanned so that we could drink the cool, sweet juice inside. In each nut there was about two and a half glassfuls of this thirst-quenching, hygienically-sealed nectar, and we savoured every mouthful.

After the rest, our next job was to get the camp in order. Two hundred yards from the village there was a small stream, and on its banks we chose an area that would not be too difficult to clear. A group of men armed with machetes set to work to cut down all the small bushes and saplings, while another group followed behind with short-handled, broad-bladed hoes, in an effort to level the red earth. At length, after the usual African uproar of insults, accusations of stupidity, sit-down strikes and minor brawls, the area had been worked over so that it resembled a badly ploughed field, and we could get the tents up. While a meal was being prepared we went down to the stream and washed the dirt and sweat from our bodies in the icy waters, watching the pink-and-brown crabs waving their pincers to us from among the rocks, and feeling the tiny, brilliant blue-and-red fish nibbling gently at our feet. We wended our way back to camp, feeling refreshed, and found some sort of organization reigning. When we had eaten, Elias came and squatted in the shade of our lean-to tent, and we discussed hunting plans.

'What time we go look dis bird, Elias?'

'Eh, Masa savvay now 'e be hot too much. For dis time dis bird 'e go look for chop for bush. For evening time when it get cold 'e go for dis 'e house for work, and den we go see um.'

'All right, then you go come back for four o'clock time, you hear? Then we go look dis bird, eh?'

'Yes, sah,' said Elias, rising to his feet.

'And if you no speak true, if we never see dis bird, if you've been funning me I go shoot you, bushman, you hear?'

'Eh!' he exclaimed, chuckling, 'I never fun with Masa, for true, sah.'

'All right, we go see you, eh?'

'Yes, sah,' he said, as he twisted his sarong round his ample hips and padded off towards the village.

At four o'clock the sun had dipped behind the tallest of the forest trees, and the air had the warm, drowsy stillness of evening. Elias returned, wearing, in place of his gaudy sarong, a scrap of dirty cloth twisted round his loins. He waved his machete nonchalantly.

'I done come, Masa,' he proclaimed. 'Masa ready?'

'Yes,' I said, shouldering my field-glasses and collecting-bag. 'Let's go, hunter man.'

Elias led us down the dusty main street of the village, and then branched off abruptly down a narrow alley-way between the huts. This led us into a small patch of farmland, full of feathery cassava bushes and dusty banana plants. Presently, the path dipped across a small stream and then wound its way into the forest. Before we had left the village street Elias had pointed out a hill to me which he said was the home of *Picathartes*, and although it had looked near enough to the village, I knew better than to believe it. The Cameroon forest is like the Looking-glass Garden. Your objective seems to loom over you, but as you walk towards it, it appears to shift position. At times, like Alice, you are forced to walk in the opposite direction in order to get there.

And so it was with this hill. The path, instead of making straight for it, seemed to weave to and fro through the forest in the most haphazard fashion, until I began to feel I must have been looking at the wrong hill when Elias had pointed it out to me. At that moment, however, the path started to climb in a determined manner, and it was obvious that we had reached the base of the hill. Elias left the path and plunged into the undergrowth on one side, hacking his way through the over-hanging lianas and thornbushes with his machete, hissing softly through his teeth, his feet spreading out in the soft leaf mould without a sound. In a very short time we were plodding up a slope so steep that, on occasions, Elias' feet were on a level with my eyes.

Most hills and mountains in the Cameroons are of a curious and exhausting construction. Created by ancient volcanic eruption, they had been pushed skywards viciously by the massive underground forces, and this has formed them in a peculiar way. They are curiously geometrical, some perfect isosceles triangles, some acute angles, some cones and some box-shaped. They rear up in such a bewildering variety of shapes that it would have been no surprise to see a cluster of them demonstrating one of the more spiky and incomprehensible of Euclid's theorems.

The hill whose sides we were now assaulting reared up in an almost perfect cone. After you had been climbing for a bit you began to gain the impression that it was much steeper than it had first appeared, and within a quarter of an hour you were convinced that the surface sloped at the rate of one in one. Elias went up it as though it were a level macadam road, ducking and weaving skilfully between the branches and overhanging undergrowth, while Bob and I, sweating and panting, struggled along behind, sometimes on all fours, in an effort to keep pace with him. Then, to our relief, just below the crest of the hill, the ground flattened out into a wide ledge, and through the tangle of trees we could see, ahead of us, a fifty-foot cliff of granite, patched with ferns and begonias, with a tumbled mass of giant, water-smoothed boulders at its base.

'Dis na de place, Masa,' said Elias, stopping and lowering his fat bottom on to a rock.

'Good,' said Bob and I in unison, and sat down to regain our breath.

When we had rested, Elias led us along through the maze of boulders to a place where the cliff face sloped outwards, overhanging the rocks below. We moved some little way along under this overhang, and then Elias stopped suddenly.

'Dere de house, Masa,' he said, his fine teeth gleaming in a grin of pride. He was pointing up at the rock face, and I saw, ten feet above us, the nest of a *Picathartes*.

At first glance it resembled a huge swallow's nest, made out of reddish-brown mud and tiny rootlets. At the base of the nest longer roots and grass stalks had been woven into the earth so that they hung down in a sort of beard; whether this was just untidy workmanship on the part of the bird, or whether it was done for reasons of camouflage, was difficult to judge. Certainly the trailing beard of roots and grass did disguise the nest, for, at first sight, it resembled nothing more than a tussock of grass and mud that had become attached to the gnarled, water-ribbed surface of the cliff. The whole nest was about the size of a football and this position under the overhang of the cliff nicely protected it from any rain.

Our first task was to discover if the nest contained anything. Luckily a tall, slender sapling was growing opposite, so we shinned up this in turn and peered into the inside of the nest. To our annoyance it was empty, though ready to receive eggs, for it had been lined with fine roots woven into a springy mat. We moved a little way along the cliff and soon came upon two more nests, one complete like the first one, and one half finished. But there was no sign of young or eggs.

'If we go hide, small time dat bird go come, sah,' said Elias.

'Are you sure?' I asked doubtfully.

'Yes, sah, for true, sah.'

'All right, we'll wait small time.'

Elias took us to a place where a cave had been scooped out of the cliff, its mouth almost blocked by an enormous boulder, and we crouched down behind this natural screen. We had a clear view of the cliff-face where the nests hung, while we ourselves were in shadow and almost hidden by the wall of stone in front of us. We settled down to wait.

The forest was getting gloomy now, for the sun was well down. The sky through the tangle of leaves and lianas above our heads was green flecked with gold, like the flanks of an enormous dragon seen between the trees. Now the very special evening noises had started. In the distance we could hear the rhythmic crash of a troupe of mona monkeys on their way to bed, leaping from tree to tree, with a sound like great surf on a rocky shore, punctuated by occasional cries of 'Oink . . .

Oink ...' from some member of the troupe. They passed
somewhere below us along the base of the hill, but the undergrowth was too thick for us to see them. Following them came
the usual retinue of hornbills, their wings making fantastically
loud whooping noises as they flew from tree to tree. Two of
them crashed into the branches above us and sat there silhou-
etted against the green sky, carrying on a long and complicated
conversation, ducking and swaying their heads, great beaks
gaping, whining and honking hysterically at each other.

Their fantastic heads, with the great beaks and sausage-shaped casques lying on top, bobbing and mowing against the sky, looked like some weird devil-masks from a Ceylonese dance.

The perpetual insect orchestra had increased a thousandfold with the approach of darkness, and the valley below us seemed to vibrate with their song. Somewhere a tree-frog started up, a long, trilling note, followed by a pause, as though he were boring a hole through a tree with a miniature pneumatic drill, and had to pause now and then to let it cool. Suddenly I heard a new noise. It was a sound I had never heard before and I glanced inquiringly at Elias. He had stiffened, and was peering into the gloomy net of lianas and leaves around us.

'Na whatee dat?' I whispered.

'Na de bird, sah.'

The first cry had been quite far down the hill, but now came another cry, much closer. It was a curious noise which can only be described, rather inadequately, as similar to the sudden sharp yap of a pekinese, but much more flute-like and plaintive. Again it came, and again, but we still could not see the bird, though we strained our eyes in the gloom.

'D'you think it's *Picathartes*?' whispered Bob.

'I don't know. . . . It's a noise I haven't heard before.'

There was a pause, and then suddenly the cry was repeated, very near now, and we lay motionless behind our rock. Not far in front of our position grew a thirty-foot sapling, bent under the weight of a liana as thick as a bell-rope that hung in loops around it, its main stem hidden in the foliage of some near-by tree. While the rest of the area we could see was gloomy and ill-defined, this sapling, lovingly entwined by its killer liana, was lit by the last rays of the setting sun, so that the whole setting was rather like a meticulous backcloth. And, as though a curtain had gone up on this miniature stage, a real live *Picathartes* suddenly appeared before us.

I say suddenly and I mean it. Animals and birds in a tropical forest generally approach so quietly that they appear before you suddenly, unexpectedly, as if dropped there by magic. The thick liana fell in a huge loop from the top of the sapling, and on this loop the bird materialized, swaying gently on its perch, its head cocked on one side as if listening. Seeing any wild animal in its natural surroundings is a thrill, but to watch something that you know is a great rarity, something that you know has only been seen by a handful of people before you, gives the whole thing an added excitement and spice. So Bob and I lay there staring at the bird with the ardent, avid expressions of a couple of philatelists who have just discovered a penny black in a child's stamp album.

The *Picathartes* was about the size of a jackdaw, but its body had the plump, sleek lines of a blackbird. Its legs were long and powerful, and its eyes large and obviously keen. The breast was a delicate creamy-buff and the back and long tail a beautiful slate grey, pale and powdery-looking. The edge of the wing was black and this acted as a dividing-line that showed up wonderfully the breast and back colours. But it was the bird's head that caught the attention and held it. It was completely bare of feathers: the forehead and top of the head were a vivid sky blue, the back a bright rose-madder pink, while the sides of the head and the cheeks were black. Normally a bald-headed bird looks rather revolting, as if it were suffering from some unpleasant and incurable disease, but *Picathartes* looked splendid with its tricoloured head, as if wearing a crown.

After the bird had perched on the liana for a minute or so it flew down on to the ground, and proceeded to work its way to and fro among the rocks in a series of prodigious leaps, quite extraordinary to watch. They were not ordinary bird-like hops, for *Picathartes* was projected into the air as if those powerful legs were springs. It disappeared from view among the rocks, and we heard it call. It was answered almost at once from the top of the cliff, and looking up we could see another *Picathartes* on a branch above us, peering down at the nests on

the cliff face. Suddenly it spiralled downwards and alighted on the edge of one of the nests, paused a moment to look about, and then leaned forward to tidy up a hair like rootlet that had become disarranged. Then the bird leaped into the air – there was no other way to describe it – and swooped down the hill into the gloomy forest. The other emerged from among the rocks and flew after it, and in a short time we heard them calling to each other plaintively among the trees.

'Ah,' said Elias, rising and stretching himself, "e done go.'

"E no go come back?' I asked, pummelling my leg, which had gone to sleep.

'No, sah. 'E done go for inside bush, for some big stick where 'e go sleep. Tomorrow 'e go come back for work dis 'e house.'

'Well, we might as well go back to Eshobi then.'

Our progress down the hill was a much speedier affair than our ascent. It was now so dark under the canopy of trees that we frequently missed our footing and slid for considerable distances on our backsides, clutching desperately at trees and roots as we passed in an effort to slow down. Eventually we emerged in the Eshobi high street bruised, scratched and covered with leaf-mould. I was filled with elation at having seen a live *Picathartes*, but, at the same time, depressed by the thought that we could not hope to get any of the youngsters. It was obviously useless hanging around in Eshobi, so I decided we would set off again for Mamfe the next day, and try to do a little collecting as we passed through the forest. One of the most successful ways of collecting animals in the Cameroons is to smoke out hollow trees, and on our way to Eshobi I had noticed several huge trees with hollow insides, which I thought might well repay investigation.

Early the next morning we packed up our equipment, and sent the carriers off with it. Then, accompanied by Elias and three other Eshobi hunters, Bob and I followed at a more leisurely pace.

The first tree was three miles into the forest, lying fairly close to the edge of the Eshobi road. It was a hundred and fifty feet high, and the greater part of its trunk was as hollow as a drum. There is quite an art to smoking out a hollow tree. It is a prolonged and sometimes complicated process. Before going to all the trouble of smoking a tree the first thing to do, if possible, is to ascertain whether or not there is anything inside worth smoking out. If the tree has a large hole at the base of the trunk, as most of them do, this is a relatively simple matter. You simply stick your head inside and get somebody to beat the trunk with a stick. If there are any animals inside you will hear them moving about uneasily after the reverberations have died away, and even if you can't hear them you can be assured of their presence by the shower of powdery rotten wood that will come cascading down the trunk. Having discovered that there is something inside the tree the next job is to scan the top part of the trunk with field-glasses and try and spot all exit holes, which then have to be covered with nets. When this has been done, a man is stationed up the tree to retrieve any creature that gets caught up there, the holes at the base of the trunk are stopped. You then light a fire, and this is the really tricky part of the operation, for the inside of these trees is generally dry and tinder-like, and if you are not careful you can set the whole thing ablaze. So first of all you kindle a small bright blaze with dry twigs, moss and leaves, and when this is well alight you carefully cover it with ever-increasing quantities of green leaves, so that the fire no longer blazes but sends up a sullen column of pungent smoke, which is sucked up the hollow barrel of the tree exactly as if it were a chimney. After this anything can happen and generally does, for these hollow trees often contain a weird variety of inhabitants, ranging from spitting cobras to civet cats, from bats to giant snails; half the charm and excitement of smoking out a tree is that you are never quite sure what is going to appear next.

The first tree we smoked was not a wild success. All we got

was a handful of leaf-nosed bats with extraordinary gargoyle-like faces, three giant millipedes that looked like Frankfurter sausages with a fringe of legs underneath and a small grey dormouse which bit one of the hunters in the thumb and escaped. So we removed the nets, put out the fire and proceeded on our way. The next hollow tree was considerably taller and of tremendous girth. At its base was an enormous split in the trunk shaped like a church door, and four of us could stand comfortably in the gloomy interior of the trunk. Peering up the hollow barrel of the trunk and beating on the wood with a machete we were rewarded by vague scuffling noises from above, and a shower of powdery rotten wood fell on our up-turned faces and into our eyes. Obviously the tree contained something. Our chief problem was to get a hunter to the top of the tree to cover the exit holes, for the trunk swept up about a hundred and twenty feet into the sky as smooth as a walking-stick. Eventually, we joined all three of our rope-ladders together, and tied a strong, light rope to one end. Then, weighting the rope end, we hurled it up and into the forest canopy until our arms ached, until at last it fell over a branch and we could haul the ladders up into the sky and secure them. So, when the nets were fixed in position at the top and bottom of the tree, we lit the fire at the base of the trunk and stood back to await results.

Generally one had to wait four or five minutes for the smoke to percolate to every part of the tree before one got any response, but in this particular case the results were almost immediate. The first beasts to appear were those nauseating-looking creatures called whip-scorpions. They cover, with their long angular legs, the area of a soup plate, and they look like a nightmare spider that has been run over by a steamroller and reduced to a paper-like thickness. This enables them to slide in and out of crevices, that would allow access to no other beast, in a most unnerving manner. Apart from this they could glide about over the surface of the wood as though it were ice, and at a speed that was quite incredible. It was this speedy and silent movement, combined with such a forest of legs, that made them so repulsive, and made one instinctively shy away from them, even though one knew they were harmless. So, when the first one appeared magically out of a crack and scuttled over my bare arm as I leant against the tree, it produced an extraordinary demoralizing effect, to say the least.

I had only just recovered from this when all the other inhabitants of the tree started to vacate in a body. Five fat grey bats flapped out into the nets, where they hung chittering madly and screwing up their faces in rage. They were quickly joined by two green forest squirrels with pale fawn rings round their eyes, who uttered shrill grunts of rage as they rolled about in the meshes of the nets while we tried to disentangle them without getting bitten. They were followed by six grey dormice, two large greeny rats with orange noses and behinds, and a slender green tree-snake with enormous eyes, who slid calmly through the meshes of the nets with a slightly affronted air, and disappeared into the undergrowth before anyone could do anything sensible about catching him. The noise and confusion was incredible: Africans danced about through the billowing smoke, shouting instructions of which nobody took the slightest notice, getting bitten with shrill yells of agony, stepping on each other's feet, wielding machetes and sticks with gay abandon and complete disregard for safety. The man posted in the top of the tree was having fun on his own, and was shouting and yelling and leaping about in the branches with such vigour that I expected to see him crash to the forest floor at any moment. Our eyes streamed, our lungs were filled with smoke, but the collecting bags filled up with a wiggling, jumping cargo of creatures.

Eventually the last of the tree's inhabitants had appeared, the smoke had died down and we could pause for a cigarette and to examine each other's honourable wounds. As we were doing this the man at the top of the tree lowered down two collecting bags on the end of long strings, before preparing to return to earth himself. I took the bags gingerly, not knowing what the contents were, and inquired of the stalwart at the top of the tree how he had fared.

'What you get for dis bag?' I inquired.

'Beef, Masa,' he replied intelligently.

'I know it's beef, bushman, but what kind of beef you get?'

'Eh! I no savvay how Masa call um. 'E so so rat, but 'e get wing. Dere be one beef for inside 'e get eye big big like man, sah.'

I was suddenly filled with an inner excitement.

''E get hand like rat or like monkey?' I shouted.

'Like monkey, sah.'

'What is it?' asked Bob with interest, as I fumbled with the string round the neck of the bags.

'I'm not sure, but I think it's a bushbaby . . . if it is it can only be one of two kinds, and both of them are rare.'

I got the string off the neck of the bag after what seemed an interminable struggle, and cautiously opened it. Regarding me from inside it was a small, neat grey face with huge ears folded back like fans against the side of the head, and two enormous golden eyes, that looked at me with the horror-stricken expression of an elderly spinster who had discovered a man in the bathroom cupboard. The creature had large, human-looking hands, with long, slender bony fingers. Each of these, except the forefinger, was tipped with a small, flat nail that looked as though it had been delicately manicured, while the forefinger possessed a curved claw that looked thoroughly out of place on such a human hand.

'What is it?' asked Bob in hushed tones, seeing that I was gazing at the creature with an expression of bliss on my face.

'This,' I said ecstatically, 'is a beast I have tried to get every time I've been to the Cameroons. *Euoticus elegantulus*, or better known as a needle-clawed lemur or bushbaby. They're extremely rare, and if we succeed in getting this one back to

England it will be the first ever to be brought back to Europe.'

'Gosh,' said Bob, suitably impressed.

I showed the little beast to Elias.

'You savvay dis beef, Elias?'

'Yes, sah, I savvay um.'

'Dis kind of beef I want *too much*. If you go get me more I go pay you one one pound. You hear.'

'I hear, sah. But Masa savvay dis kind of beef 'e come out for night time. For dis kind of beef you go look um with hunter light.'

'Yes, but you tell all people of Eshobi I go pay one one pound for dis beef, you hear?'

'Yes, sah. I go tell um.'

'And now,' I said to Bob, carefully tying up the bag with the precious beef inside, 'let's get back to Mamfe quick and get this into a decent cage where we can see it.'

So we packed up the equipment and set off at a brisk pace through the forest towards Mamfe, pausing frequently to open the bag and make sure that the precious specimen had got enough air, and had not been spirited away by some frightful juju. We reached Mamfe at lunch-time and burst into the house, calling to Jacquie and Sophie to come and see our prize. I opened the bag cautiously and *Euoticus* edged its head out and surveyed us all in turn with its enormous, staring eyes.

'Oh, isn't it *sweet*,' said Jacquie.

'Isn't it a *dear*?' said Sophie.

'Yes,' I said proudly, 'it's a . . .'

'What shall we call it?' asked Jacquie.

'We'll have to think of a good name for it,' said Sophie.

'It's an extremely rare . . .' I began.

'How about Bubbles?' suggested Sophie.

'No, it doesn't look like a Bubbles,' said Jacquie surveying it critically.

'It's an *Euoticus* . . .'

'How about Moony?'

'No one has ever taken it back . . .'

'No, it doesn't look like a Moony either.'

'No European zoo has ever . . .'

'What about Fluffykins?' asked Sophie.

I shuddered.

'If you must give it a name call it Bug-eyes,' I said.

'Oh, yes!' said Jacquie, 'that suits it.'

'Good,' I said, 'I am relieved to know that we have successfully christened it. Now what about a cage for it?'

'Oh, we've got one here,' said Jacquie. 'Don't worry about that.'

We eased the animal into the cage, and it squatted on the floor glaring at us with unabated horror.

'Isn't it sweet?' Jacquie repeated.

'Is 'o a poppet?' gurgled Sophie.

I sighed. It seemed that, in spite of all my careful training, both my wife and my secretary relapsed into the most revolting fubsy attitude when faced with anything fluffy.

'Well,' I said resignedly, 'supposing you feed 'oos poppet? This poppet's going inside to get an itsy-bitsy slug of gin.'

PART TWO

BACK TO BAFUT

MAIL BY HAND

My good friend,
   I am glad that you have arrive once more to Bafut. I welcome you. When you are calm from your journeys come and see me.

Your good friend,
Fon of Bafut.

CHAPTER THREE

THE FON'S BEEF

ON our return from Eshobi, Jacquie and I loaded up our lorry with the cages of animals we had obtained to date, and set out for Bafut, leaving Bob and Sophie in Mamfe for a little longer to try and obtain some more of the rain-forest animals.

The journey from Mamfe to the highlands was long and tedious, but never failed to fascinate me. To begin with, the road ran through the thick forest of the valley in which Mamfe lay. The lorry roared and bumped its way along the red road between gigantic trees, each festooned with creepers and lianas, through which flew small flocks of hornbills, honking wildly, or pairs of jade-green touracos with magenta wings flashing as they flew. On the dead trees by the side of the road the lizards, orange, blue and black, vied with the pigmy king-fishers over the spiders, locusts and other succulent titbits to be found amongst the purple and white convolvulus flowers. At the bottom of each tiny valley ran a small stream, spanned by a creaking wooden bridge, and as the lorry roared across, great clouds of butterflies rose from the damp earth at the sides of the water and swirled briefly round the bonnet. After a couple of hours the road started to climb, at first almost imperceptibly, in a series of great swinging loops through the forest, and here and there by the side of the road you could see the giant tree-ferns like green fountains spouting miraculously out of the low growth. As one climbed higher, the forest gave way to occasional patches of grassland, bleached white by the sun.

Then, gradually, as though we were shedding a thick green coat, the forest started to drop away and the grassland took its place. The gay lizards ran sun-drunk across the road, and flocks of minute finches burst from the undergrowth and drifted across in front of us, their crimson feathering making them look like showers of sparks from some gigantic bonfire. The lorry roared and shuddered, steam blowing up from the radiator, as it made the final violent effort and reached the top of the escarpment. Behind lay the Mamfe forest, in a million shades of green, and before us was the grassland, hundreds of miles of rolling mountains, lying in folds to the farthest dim horizons, gold and green, stroked by cloud shadows, remote and beautiful in the sun. The driver eased the lorry on to the top of the hill and brought it to a shuddering halt that made the red dust swirl up in a waterspout that enveloped us and our belongings. He smiled the wide, happy smile of a man who has accomplished something of importance.

'Why we stop?' I inquired.

'I go piss,' explained the driver frankly, as he disappeared into the long grass at the side of the road.

Jacquie and I uncoiled ourselves from the red-hot interior of the cab and walked round to the back of the lorry to see how our creatures were faring. Phillip, seated stiff and upright on a tarpaulin, turned to us a face bright red with dust. His trilby, which had been a very delicate pearl grey when we started, was also bright red. He sneezed violently into a green handkerchief, and surveyed me reproachfully.

'Dust *too much*, sah,' he roared at me, in case the fact had escaped my observation. As Jacquie and I were almost as dusty in the front of the lorry, I was not inclined to be sympathetic.

'How are the animals?' I asked.

''E well, sah. But dis bush-hog, sah, 'e get strong head *too much*.'

'Why, what the matter with it?'

''E done tief dis ma pillow,' said Phillip indignantly.

I peered into Ticky, the black-footed mongoose's cage. She had whiled away the tedium of the journey by pushing her paw through the bars and gradually dragging in with her the small pillow which was part of our cook's bedding. She was sitting on the remains, looking very smug and pleased with herself, surrounded by snow-drifts of feathers.

'Never mind,' I said consolingly, 'I'll buy you a new one. But you go watch your other things, eh? Sometime she go tief them as well.'

'Yes, sah, I go watch um,' said Phillip, casting a black look at the feather-smothered Ticky.

So we drove on through the green, gold and white grassland, under a blue sky veined with fine wisps of wind-woven white cloud, like frail twists of sheep's wool blowing across the sky. Everything in this landscape seemed to be the work of the wind. The great outcrops of grey rocks were carved and ribbed by it into fantastic shapes; the long grass was curved over into frozen waves by it; the small trees had been bent, carunculated and distorted by it. And the whole landscape throbbed and sang with the wind, hissing softly in the grass, making the small trees creak and whine, hooting and blaring round the towering cornices of rock.

So we drove on towards Bafut, and towards the end of the day the sky became pale gold. Then, as the sun sank behind the farthest rim of mountains, the world was enveloped in the cool green twilight, and in the dusk the lorry roared round the last bend and drew up at the hub of Bafut, the compound of the Fon. To the left lay the vast courtyard, and behind it the clusters of huts in which lived the Fon's wives and children. Dominating them all was the great hut in which dwelt the spirit of his father, and a great many other lesser spirits, looming like a monstrous, time-blackened beehive against the jade night sky. To the right of the road, perched on top of a tall bank, was the Fon's Rest House, like a two-storey Italian villa, stone-built and with a neatly tiled roof. Shoe-box shaped, both lower and upper storeys were surrounded by wide verandahs, festooned with bougainvillaea covered with pink and brick-red flowers.

Tiredly we climbed out of the lorry and supervised the unloading of the animals and their installation on the top-storey verandah. Then the rest of the equipment was off-loaded and stored, and while we made vague attemps to wash some of the red dust off our bodies, Phillip seized the remains of his bedding, his box full of cooking utensils and food and marched off to the kitchen quarters in a stiff, brisk way, like a military patrol going to quell a small but irritating insurrection. By the time we had fed the animals he had reappeared with an astonishingly good meal and having eaten it we fell into bed and slept like the dead.

The next morning, in the cool dawn light, we went to pay our respects to our host, the Fon. We made our way across the great courtyard and plunged into the maze of tiny squares and alleyways formed by the huts of the Fon's wives. Presently, we found ourselves in a small courtyard shaded by an immense guava tree, and there was the Fon's own villa, small, neat, built of stone and tiled with a wide verandah running along one side. And there, at the top of the steps running up to the verandah, stood my friend the Fon of Bafut.

He stood there, tall and slender, wearing a plain white robe embroidered with blue. On his head was a small skull-cap in the same colours. His face was split by the joyous, mischievous grin I knew so well and he was holding out one enormous slender hand in greeting.

'My friend, Iseeya,' I called, hurrying up the stairs to him.

'Welcome, welcome ... you done come ... welcome,' he exclaimed, seizing my hand in his huge palm and draping a long arm round my shoulders and patting me affectionately.

'You well, my friend?' I asked, peering up into his face.

'I well, I well,' he said grinning.

It seemed to me an understatement: he looked positively blooming. He had been well into his seventies when I had last met him, eight years before, and he appeared to have weathered the intervening years better than I had. I introduced Jacquie, and was quietly amused by the contrast. The Fon, six foot three inches, and appearing taller because of his robes, towered beamingly over Jacquie's five-foot-one-inch, and her hand was as lost as a child's in the depths of his great dusky paw.

'Come, we go for inside,' he said, and clutching our hands led us into his villa.

The interior was as I remembered it, a cool, pleasant room with leopard skins on the floor, and wooden sofas, beautifully carved, piled high with cushions. We sat down, and one of the Fon's wives came forward carrying a tray with glasses and drinks on it. The Fon splashed Scotch into three glasses with a liberal hand, and passed them round, beaming at us. I surveyed the four inches of neat spirit in the bottom of my glass and sighed. I could see that the Fon had not, in my absence, joined the Temperance movement, whatever else he had done.

'Chirri-ho!' said the Fon, and downed half the contents of his glass at a gulp. Jacquie and I sipped ours more sedately.

'My friend,' I said, 'I happy too much I see you again.'

'Wah! Happy?' said the Fon. 'I get happy for see you. When dey done tell me you come for Cameroon again I get happy too much.'

I sipped my drink cautiously.

'Some man done tell me that you get angry for me because

I done write dat book about dis happy time we done have together before. So I de fear for come back to Bafut,' I said.

The Fon scowled.

'Which kind of man tell you dis ting?' he inquired furiously.

'Some European done tell me.'

'Ah! European,' said the Fon shrugging, as if surprised that I should believe anything told to me by a white person, 'Na lies dis.'

'Good,' I said, greatly relieved. 'If I think you get angry for me my heart no go be happy.'

'No, no, I no get angry for you,' said the Fon, splashing another large measure of Scotch into my glass before I could stop him. 'Dis book you done write . . . I like um foine . . . you done make my name go for all de world . . . every kind of people 'e know my name . . . na foine ting dis.'

Once again I realized I had underestimated the Fon's abilities. He had obviously realized that any publicity is better than none. 'Look um,' he went on, 'plenty plenty people come here for Bafut, all different different people, dey all show me dis your book 'e get my name for inside . . . na foine ting dis.'

'Yes, na fine thing,' I agreed, rather shaken. I had had no idea that I had unwittingly turned the Fon into a sort of Literary Lion.

'Dat time I done go for Nigeria,' he said, pensively holding the bottle of Scotch up to the light. 'Dat time I done go for Lagos to meet dat Queen woman, all dis European dere 'e get dis your book. Plenty plenty people dey ask me for write dis ma name for inside dis your book.'

I gazed at him open-mouthed; the idea of the Fon in Lagos sitting and autographing copies of my book rendered me speechless.

'Did you like the Queen?' asked Jacquie.

'Wah! Like? I like um too much. Na foine woman dat. Na small small woman, same same for you. But 'e get power, time no dere. Wah! Dat woman get power *plenty*.'

'Did you like Nigeria?' I asked.

'I no like,' said the Fon firmly. ''E hot too much. Sun, sun, sun, I shweat, I shweat. But dis Queen woman she get plenty power . . . she walka walka she never shweat. Na foine woman dis.'

He chuckled reminiscently, and absent-mindedly poured us all out another drink.

'I done give dis Queen,' he went on, 'dis teeth for elephant. You savvay um?'

'Yes, I savvay um,' I said, remembering the magnificent carved tusk the Cameroons had presented to Her Majesty.

'I done give dis teeth for all dis people of Cameroon,' he explained. 'Dis Queen she sit for some chair an' I go softly softly for give her dis teeth. She take um. Den all dis European dere dey say it no be good ting for show your arse for dis Queen woman, so all de people walka walka backwards. I walka walka backwards. Wah! Na step dere, eh! I de fear I de fall, but I walka walka softly and I never fall . . . but I de fear too much.'

He chuckled over the memory of himself backing down the steps in front of the Queen until his eyes filled with tears.

'Nigeria no be good place,' he said, 'hot too much . . . I shweat.'

At the mention of sweat I saw his eyes fasten on the whisky bottle, so I rose hurriedly to my feet and said that we really ought to be going, as we had a lot of unpacking to do. The Fon walked out into the sunlit courtyard with us, and, holding our hands, peered earnestly down into our faces.

'For evening time you go come back,' he said. 'We go drink, eh?'

'Yes, for evening time we go come,' I assured him.

He beamed down at Jacquie.

'For evening time I go show you what kind of happy time we get for Bafut,' he said.

'Good,' said Jacquie, smiling bravely.

The Fon waved his hands in elegant dismissal, and then turned and made his way back into his villa, while we trudged over to the Rest House.

'I don't think I could face any breakfast after that Scotch,' said Jacquie.

'But that wasn't drinking,' I protested. 'That was just a sort of mild apéritif to start the day. You wait until tonight.'

'Tonight I shan't drink . . . I'll leave it to you two,' said Jacquie firmly. 'I shall have one drink and that's all.'

After breakfast, while we were attending to the animals, I happened to glance over the verandah rail and noticed on the road below a small group of men approaching the house. When they drew nearer I saw that each of them was carrying either a raffia basket or a calabash with the neck stuffed with green leaves. I could hardly believe that they were bringing animals as soon as this, for generally it takes anything up to a week for the news to get around and for the hunters to start bringing in the stuff. But as I watched them with bated breath they turned off the road and started to climb the long flight of steps up to the verandah, chattering and laughing among themselves. Then, when they reached the top step they fell silent, and carefully laid their offerings on the ground.

'Iseeya, my friends,' I said.

'Morning, Masa,' they chorused, grinning.

'Na whatee all dis ting?'

'Na beef, sah,' they said.

'But how you savvay dat I done come for Bafut for buy beef?' I asked, greatly puzzled.

'Eh, Masa, de Fon 'e done tell us,' said one of the hunters.

'Good lord, if the Fon's been spreading the news before we arrived we'll be inundated in next to no time,' said Jacquie.

'We're pretty well inundated now,' I said, surveying the group of containers at my feet, 'and we haven't even unpacked the cages yet. Oh well, I suppose we'll manage. Let's see what they've got.'

I bent down, picked up a raffia bag and held it aloft.

'Which man bring dis?' I asked.

'Na me, sah.'

'Na whatee dere for inside?'

'Na squill-lill, sah.'

'What,' inquired Jacquie, as I started to unravel the strings on the bag, 'is a squill-lill?'

'I haven't the faintest idea,' I replied.

'Well, hadn't you better ask?' suggested Jacquie practically. 'For all you know it might be a cobra or something.'

'Yes, that's a point,' I agreed, pausing.

I turned to the hunter who was watching me anxiously.

'Na whatee dis beef squill-lill?'

'Na small beef, sah.'

'Na, bad beef? 'E go chop man?'

'No, sah, at all. Dis one na squill-lill small, sah . . . na picken.'

Fortified with this knowledge I opened the bag and peered into its depths. At the bottom, squirming and twitching in a nest of grass, lay a tiny squirrel about three and a half inches long. It couldn't have been more than a few days old, for it was still covered in the neat, shining plush-like fur of an infant, and it was still blind. I lifted it out carefully and it lay in my hand making faint squeaking noises like something out of a Christmas cracker, pink mouth open in an O like a choirboy's, minute paws making paddling motions against my fingers. I waited patiently for the flood of anthropomorphism to die down from my wife.

'Well,' I said, 'if you want it, keep it. But I warn you it will be hell to feed. The only reason I can see for trying is because its a baby black-eared, and they're quite rare.'

'Oh, it'll be all right,' said Jacquie optimistically. 'It's strong and that's half the battle.'

I sighed. I remembered the innumerable baby squirrels I had struggled with in various parts of the world, and how each one had seemed more imbecile and more bent on self-destruction than the last. I turned to the hunter. 'Dis beef, my friend. Na fine beef dis, I like um too much. But 'e be picken, eh? Some time 'e go die-o, eh?'

'Yes, sah,' agreed the hunter gloomily.

'So I go pay you two two shilling now, and I go give you book. You go come back for two week time, eh, and if dis picken 'e alive I go pay you five five shilling more, eh? You agree?'

'Yes, sah, I agree,' said the hunter, grinning delightedly.

I paid him the two shillings, and then wrote out a promissory note for the other five shillings, and watched him tuck it carefully into a fold of his sarong.

'You no go lose um,' I said. 'If you go lose um I no go pay you.'

'No, Masa, I no go lose um,' he assured me, grinning.

'You know, it's the most beautiful colour,' said Jacquie, peering at the squirrel in her cupped hands. On that point I agreed with her. The diminutive head was bright orange, with a neat black rim behind each ear, as though its mother had not washed it properly. The body was brindled green on the back and pale yellow on the tummy, while the ridiculous tail was darkish green above and flame orange below.

'What shall I call it?' asked Jacquie.

I glanced at the quivering scrap, still doing choral practice in her palm.

'Call it what the hunter called it: Squill-lill Small,' I suggested. So Squill-lill Small she became, later to be abbreviated to Small for convenience.

While engaged in this problem of nomenclature I had been busy untying another raffia basket, without having taken the precaution of asking the hunter what it contained. So, when I incautiously opened it, a small, pointed, rat-like face appeared, bit me sharply on the finger, uttered a piercing shriek of rage and disappeared into the depths of the basket again.

'What on earth was that?' asked Jacquie, as I sucked my

finger and cursed, while all the hunters chorused 'Sorry, sah, sorry, sah,' as though they had been collectively responsible for my stupidity.

'That fiendish little darling is a pigmy mongoose,' I said. 'For their size they're probably the fiercest creatures in Bafut, and they've got the most penetrating scream of any small animal I know, except a marmoset.'

'What are we going to keep it in?'

'We'll have to unpack some cages. I'll leave it in the bag until I've dealt with the rest of the stuff,' I said, carefully tying the bag up again.

'It's nice to have two different species of mongoose,' said Jacquie.

'Yes,' I agreed, sucking my finger. 'Delightful.'

The rest of the containers, when examined, yielded nothing more exciting than three common toads, a small green viper and four weaver-birds which I did not want. So, having disposed of them and the hunters, I turned my attention to the task of housing the pigmy mongoose. One of the worst things you can do on a collecting trip is to be unprepared with your caging. I had made this mistake on my first expedition; although we had taken a lot of various equipment, I had failed to include any ready-made cages, thinking there would be plenty of time to build them on the spot. The result was that the first flood of animals caught us unprepared and by the time we had struggled night and day to house them all adequately, the second wave of creatures had arrived and we were back where we started. At one point I had as many as six different creatures tied to my camp-bed on strings. After this experience I have always taken the precaution of bringing some collapsible cages with me on a trip so that, whatever else happens, I am certain I can accommodate at least the first forty or fifty specimens.

I now erected one of our specially built cages, filled it with dry banana leaves and eased the pigmy mongoose into it without getting bitten. It stood in the centre of the cage, regarding me with small, bright eyes, one dainty paw held up, and proceeded to utter shriek upon shriek of fury until our ears throbbed. The noise was so penetrating and painful that, in desperation, I threw a large lump of meat into the cage. The pigmy leaped on it, shook it vigorously to make sure it was dead and then carried it off to a corner where it settled down to eat. Though it still continued to shriek at us, the sounds were now mercifully muffled by the food. I placed the cage next to the one occupied by Ticky, the black-footed mongoose, and sat down to watch.

At a casual glance no one would think that the two animals were even remotely related. The black-footed mongoose, although still only a baby, measured two feet in length and stood about eight inches in height. She had a blunt, rather dog-like face with dark, round and somewhat protuberant eyes. Her body, head and tail were a rich creamy-white, while her slender legs were a rich brown that was almost black. She was sleek, sinuous and svelte and reminded me of a soft-skinned Parisienne *belle-amie* clad in nothing more than two pairs of black silk stockings. In contrast the pigmy mongoose looked anything but Parisienne. It measured, including tail, about ten inches in length. It had a tiny, sharply pointed face with a small, circular pink nose and a pair of small, glittering, sherry-coloured eyes. The fur, which was rather long and thick, was a deep chocolate brown with a faint ginger tinge here and there.

Ticky, who was very much the *grande dame*, peered out of her cage at the newcomer with something akin to horror on her face, watching it fascinated as it shrieked and grumbled over its gory hunk of meat. Ticky was herself a very dainty and fastidious feeder and would never have dreamt of behaving in this uncouth way, yelling and screaming with your mouth full and generally carrying on as though you had never had a square meal in your life. She watched the pigmy for a moment or so and then gave a sniff of scorn, turned round elegantly two or three times and then lay down and went to sleep. The pigmy, undeterred by this comment on its behaviour, continued to champ and shrill over the last bloody remnants of its food. When the last morsel had been gulped down, and the ground around carefully inspected for any bits that might have been overlooked, it sat down and scratched itself vigorously for a while and then curled up and went to sleep as well. When we woke it up about an hour later to record its voice for posterity, it produced such screams of rage and indignation that we were forced to move the microphone to the other end of the verandah. But by the time evening came we had not only successfully recorded the pigmy mongoose but Ticky as well, and had unpacked ninety per cent of our equipment into the bargain. So we bathed, changed and dined feeling well satisfied with ourselves.

After dinner we armed ourselves with a bottle of whisky and an abundant supply of cigarettes and, taking our pressure-lamp, we set off for the Fon's house. The air was warm and drowsy, full of the scents of wood smoke and sun-baked earth. Crickets tinkled and trilled in the grass verges of the road and in the gloomy fruit-trees around the Fon's great courtyard we could hear the fruit bats honking and flapping their wings among the branches. In the courtyard a group of the Fon's children were standing in a circle clapping their hands and chanting in some sort of game, and away through the trees in the distance a small drum throbbed like an irregular heart beat. We made our way through the maze of wives' huts, each lit by the red glow of a cooking fire, each heavy with the smell of roasting yams, frying plantain, stewing meat or the sharp, pungent reek of dried salt fish. We came presently to the Fon's villa and he was waiting on the steps to greet us, looming large in the gloom, his robe swishing as he shook our hands.

'Welcome, welcome,' he said, beaming, 'come, we go for inside.'

'I done bring some whisky for make our heart happy,' I said, flourishing the bottle as we entered the house.

'Wah! Good, good,' said the Fon, chuckling. 'Dis whisky na foine ting for make man happy.'

He was wearing a wonderful scarlet-and-yellow robe that glowed like a tiger skin in the soft lamplight, and one slender wrist carried a thick, beautifully carved ivory bracelet. We sat down and waited in silence while the solemn ritual of the pouring of the first drink was observed. Then, when each of us was clutching half a tumbler full of neat whisky, the Fon turned to us, giving his wide, mischievous grin.

'Chirri-*ho*!' he said, raising his glass ,'tonight we go have happy time.' And so began what we were to refer to later as The Evening of the Hangover.

As the level in the whisky bottle fell the Fon told us once again about his trip to Nigeria, how hot it had been and how much he had 'shweated'. His praise for the Queen knew no bounds, for, as he pointed out, here was he in his own country feeling the heat and yet the Queen could do twice the amount of work and still manage to look cool and charming. I found his lavish and perfectly genuine praise rather extraordinary, for the Fon belonged to a society where women are considered to be nothing more than rather useful beasts of burden.

'You like musica?' inquired the Fon of Jacquie, when the subject of the Nigerian tour was exhausted.

'Yes,' said Jacquie, 'I like it very much.'

The Fon beamed at her.

'You remember dis my musica?' he asked me.

'Yes, I remember. You get musica time no dere, my friend.'

The Fon gave a prolonged crow of amusement.

'You done write about dis my musica inside dis your book, eh?'

'Yes, that's right.'

'And,' said the Fon, coming to the point, 'you done write about dis dancing an' dis happy time we done have, eh?'

'Yes . . . all dis dance we done do na fine one.'

'You like we go show dis your wife what kind of dance we get here for Bafut?' he inquired, pointing a long forefinger at me.

'Yes, I like too much.'

'Foine, foine . . . come, we go for dancing house,' he said, rising to his feet majestically, and stifling a belch with one slender hand. Two of his wives, who had been sitting quietly in the background, rushed forward and seized the tray of drinks and scuttled ahead of us, as the Fon led us out of his house and across the compound towards his dancing house.

The dancing house was a great, square building, not unlike the average village hall, but with an earth floor and very few and very small windows. At one end of the building stood a line of wickerwork arm-chairs, which constituted a sort of Royal enclosure, and on the wall above these were framed photographs of various members of the Royal family. As we entered the dancing hall the assembled wives, about forty or fifty of them, uttered the usual greeting, a strange, shrill ululation, caused by yelling loudly and clapping their hands rapidly over their mouths at the same time. The noise was deafening. All the petty councillors there in their brilliant robes clapped their hands as well, and thus added to the general racket. Nearly deafened by this greeting, Jacquie and I were installed in two chairs, one on each side of the Fon, the table of drinks was placed in front of us, and the Fon, leaning back in his chair, surveyed us both with a wide and happy grin.

'Now we go have happy time,' he said, and leaning forward poured out half a tumblerful of Scotch each from the depths of a virgin bottle that had just been broached.

'Chirri-ho,' said the Fon.

'Chin-chin,' I said absent-mindedly.

'Na whatee dat?' inquired the Fon with interest.

'What?' I asked, puzzled.

'Dis ting you say.'

'Oh, you mean chin-chin?'

'Yes, yes, dis one.'

'It's something you say when you drink.'

'Na same same for Chirri-ho?' asked the Fon, intrigued.

'Yes, na same same.'

He sat silent for a moment, his lips moving, obviously comparing the respective merits of the two toasts. Then he raised his glass again.

'Shin-shin,' said the Fon.

'Chirri-ho!' I responded, and the Fon lay back in his chair and went off into a paroxysm of mirth.

By now the band had arrived. It was composed of four youths and two of the Fon's wives and the instruments consisted of three drums, two flutes and a calabash filled with dried maize that gave off a pleasant rustling noise similar to a marimba. They got themselves organized in the corner of the dancing house, and then gave a few experimental rolls on the drums, watching the Fon expectantly. The Fon, having recovered from the joke, barked out an imperious order and two of his wives placed a small table in the centre of the dance floor and put a pressure lamp on it. The drums gave another expectant roll.

'My friend,' said the Fon, 'you remember when you done come for Bafut before you done teach me European dance, eh?'

'Yes,' I said, 'I remember.'

This referred to one of the Fon's parties when, having partaken liberally of the Fon's hospitality, I had proceeded to show him, his councillors and wives how to do the conga. It had been a riotous success, but in the eight years that had passed I had supposed that the Fon would have forgotten about it.

'I go show you,' said the Fon, his eyes gleaming. He barked out another order and about twenty of his wives shuffled out on to the dance floor and formed a circle round the table, each one holding firmly to the waist of the one in front. Then they assumed a strange, crouching position, rather like runners at the start of a race, and waited.

'What are they going to do?' whispered Jacquie.

I watched them with an unholy glee. 'I do believe,' I said dreamily, 'that he's been making them dance the conga ever since I left, and we're now going to have a demonstration.'

The Fon lifted a large hand and the band launched itself with enthusiasm into a Bafut tune that had the unmistakable conga rhythm. The Fon's wives, still in their strange crouching position, proceeded to circle round the lamp, kicking their black legs out on the sixth beat, their brows furrowed in concentration. The effect was delightful.

'My friend,' I said, touched by the demonstration, 'dis na fine ting you do.'

'Wonderful,' agreed Jacquie enthusiastically, 'they dance very fine.'

'Dis na de dance you done teach me,' explained the Fon.

'Yes, I remember.'

He turned to Jacquie, chuckling. 'Dis man your husband 'e get plenty power . . . we dance, we dance, we drink . . . Wah! We done have happy time.'

The band came to an uneven halt, and the Fon's wives, smiling shyly at our applause, rose from their crouching position and returned to their former places along the wall. The Fon barked an order and a large calabash of palm wine was brought in and distributed among the dancers, each getting their share poured into their cupped hands. Stimulated by this sight the Fon filled all our glasses again.

'Yes,' he went on, reminiscently, 'dis man your husband get plenty power for dance and drink.'

'I no get power now,' I said, 'I be old man now.'

'No, no, my friend,' said the Fon laughing, 'I be old, you be young.'

'You look more young now den for the other time I done come to Bafut,' I said, and really meant it.

'That's because you've got plenty wives,' said Jacquie.

'Wah! No' said the Fon, shocked. 'Dis ma wives tire me too much.'

He glared moodily at the array of females standing along the wall, and sipped his drink. 'Dis ma wife dey humbug me too much,' he went on.

'My husband says I humbug him,' said Jacquie.

'Your husband catch lucky. 'E only get one wife, I get plenty,' said the Fon, 'an' dey de humbug me time no dere.'

'But wives are very useful,' said Jacquie.

The Fon regarded her sceptically.

'If you don't have wives you can't have *babies* ... men can't have babies,' said Jacquie practically.

The Fon was so overcome with mirth at this remark I thought he might have a stroke. He lay back in his chair and laughed until he cried. Presently he sat up, wiping his eyes, still shaking with gusts of laughter. 'Dis woman your wife get brain,' he said, still chuckling, and poured Jacquie out an extra large Scotch to celebrate her intelligence. 'You be good wife for me,' he said, patting her on the head affectionately. 'Shin-shin.'

The band now returned, wiping their mouths from some mysterious errand outside the dancing house and, apparently well fortified, launched themselves into one of my favourite Bafut tunes, the Butterfly dance. This was a pleasant, lilting little tune and the Fon's wives again took the floor and did the delightful dance that accompanied it. They danced in a row with minute but complicated hand and feet movements, and then the two that formed the head of the line joined hands, while the one at the farther end of the line whirled up and then fell backwards, to be caught and thrown upright again by the two with linked hands. As the dance progressed and the music got faster and faster the one representing the butterfly whirled more and more rapidly, and the ones with linked hands catapulted her upright again with more and more enthusiasm. Then, when the dance reached its feverish climax, the Fon rose majestically to his feet, amid screams of delight from the audience, and joined the end of the row of dancing wives. He started to whirl down the line, his scarlet and yellow robe turning into a blur of colour, loudly singing the words of the song.

'I dance, I dance, and no one can stop me,' he carolled merrily, 'but I must take care not to fall to the ground like the butterfly.'

He went whirling down the line of wives like a top, his voice booming out above theirs.

'I hope to God they don't drop him,' I said to Jacquie, eyeing the two short, fat wives who, with linked hands, were waiting rather nervously at the head of the line to receive their lord and master.

The Fon performed one last mighty gyration and hurled himself backwards at his wives, who caught him neatly enough but reeled under the shock. As the Fon landed he spread his arms wide so that for a moment his wives were invisible under the flowing sleeves of his robes and he lay there looking very like a gigantic, multicoloured butterfly. He beamed at us, lolling across his wives arms, his skull-cap slightly askew, and then his wives with an effort bounced him back to his feet again. Grinning and panting he made his way back to us and hurled himself into his chair.

'My friend, na fine dance dis,' I said in admiration. 'You get power time no dere.'

'Yes,' agreed Jacquie, who had also been impressed by this display, 'you get plenty power.'

'Na good dance dis, na foine one,' said the Fon, chuckling, and automatically pouring us all out another drink.

'You get another dance here for Bafut I like too much,' I said. 'Dis one where you dance with dat beer-beer for horse.'

'Ah, yes, yes, I savvay um,' said the Fon. 'Dat one where we go dance with dis tail for horshe.'

'That's right. Sometime, my friend, you go show dis dance for my wife?'

'Yes, yes, my friend,' he said. He leant forward and gave an order and a wife scuttled out of the dancing hall. The Fon turned and smiled at Jacquie.

'Small time dey go bring dis tail for horshe an' den we go dance,' he said.

Presently the wife returned carrying a large bundle of white, silky horses tails, each about two feet long, fitted into handles beautifully woven out of leather thongs. The Fon's tail was a particularly long and luxuriant one, and the thongs that had been used to make the handle were dyed blue, red and gold. The Fon swished it experimentally through the air with languid, graceful movements of his wrist, and the hair rippled and floated like a cloud of smoke before him. Twenty of the Fon's wives, each armed with a switch, took the floor and formed a circle. The Fon walked over and stood in the centre of the circle; he gave a wave of his horse's tail, the band struck up and the dance was on.

Of all the Bafut dances this horsetail dance was undoubtedly the most sensuous and beautiful. The rhythm was peculiar, the small drums keeping up a sharp, staccato beat, while beneath them the big drums rumbled and muttered and the bamboo flutes squeaked and twittered with a tune that seemed to have nothing to do with the drums and yet merged with it perfectly. To this tune the Fon's wives gyrated slowly round in a clockwise direction, their feet performing minute but formalized steps, while they waved the horses' tails gently to and fro across their faces. The Fon, meanwhile, danced round the inside of the circle in an anti-clockwise direction, bobbing, stamping and twisting in a curiously stiff, unjointed sort of way, while his hand with incredibly supple wrist movements kept his horse's tail waving through the air in a series of lovely and complicated movements. The effect was odd and almost indescribable: one minute the dancers resembled a bed of white seaweed, moved and rippled by sea movement, and the next minute the Fon would stamp and twist, stiff-legged, like some strange bird with white plumes, absorbed in a ritual dance of courtship among his circle of hens. Watching this slow pavane and the graceful movements of the tails had a curious hypnotic effect, so that even when the dance ended with a roll of drums one could still see the white tails weaving and merging before your eyes.

The Fon moved gracefully across the floor towards us, twirling his horse's tail negligently, and sank into his seat. He beamed breathlessly at Jacquie.

'You like dis ma dance?' he asked.

'It was *beautiful*,' she said. 'I liked it very much.'

'Good, good,' said the Fon, well pleased. He leaned forward and inspected the whisky bottle hopefully, but it was obviously empty. Tactfully I refrained from mentioning that I had some more over at the Rest House. The Fon surveyed the bottle gloomily.

'Whisky done finish,' he pointed out.

'Yes,' I said unhelpfully.

'Well,' said the Fon, undaunted, 'we go drink gin.'

My heart sank, for I had hoped that we could now move on to something innocuous like beer to quell the effects of so much neat alcohol. The Fon roared at one of his wives and she ran off and soon reappeared with a bottle of gin and one of bitters. The Fon's idea of gin-drinking was to pour out half a tumblerful and then colour it a deep brown with bitters. The result was guaranteed to slay an elephant at twenty paces. Jacquie, on seeing this cocktail the Fon concocted for me, hastily begged to be excused, saying that she couldn't drink gin on doctor's orders. The Fon, though obviously having the lowest possible opinion of a medical man who could even suggest such a thing, accepted with good grace.

The band started up again and everyone poured on to the floor and started to dance, singly and in couples. As the rhythm of the tune allowed it, Jacquie and I got up and did a swift foxtrot round the floor, the Fon roaring encouragement and his wives hooting with pleasure.

'Foine, foine,' shouted the Fon as we swept past.

'Thank you, my friend,' I shouted back, steering Jacquie carefully through what looked like a flower-bed of councillors in their multicoloured robes.

'I do wish you wouldn't tread on my feet,' said Jacquie plaintively.

'Sorry. My compass bearings are never at their best at this hour of night.'

'So I notice,' said Jacquie acidly.

'Why don't you dance with the Fon?' I inquired.

'I did think of it, but I wasn't sure whether it was the right thing for a mere woman to ask him.'

'I think he'd be tickled pink. Ask him for the next dance,' I suggested.

'What can we dance?' asked Jacquie.

'Teach him something he can add to his Latin American repertoire,' I said. 'How about a rumba?'

'I think a samba would be easier to learn at this hour of night,' said Jacquie. So, when the dance ended we made our way back to where the Fon was sitting, topping up my glass.

'My friend,' I said, 'you remember dis European dance I done teach you when I done come for Bafut before?'

'Yes, yes, na foine one,' he replied, beaming.

'Well, my wife like to dance with you and teach you other European dance. You agree?'

'Wah!' bellowed the Fon in delight, 'foine, foine. Dis your wife go teach me. Foine, foine, I agree.'

Eventually we discovered a tune that the band could play that had a vague samba rhythm and Jacquie and the Fon rose to their feet, watched breathlessly by everyone in the room.

The contrast between the Fon's six-foot-three and Jacquie's five-foot-one made me choke over my drink as they took the floor. Very rapidly Jacquie showed him the simple, basic steps of the samba, and to my surprise the Fon mastered them without trouble. Then he seized Jacquie in his arms and they were off. The delightful thing from my point of view was that as he clasped Jacquie tightly to his bosom she was almost completely hidden by his flowing robes; indeed, at some points in the dance you could not see her at all and it looked as though the Fon, having mysteriously grown another pair of feet, was dancing round by himself. There was something else about the dance that struck me as curious, but I could not pin it

down for some time. Then I suddenly realized that Jacquie was leading the Fon. They danced past, both grinning at me, obviously hugely enjoying themselves.

'You dance fine, my friend,' I shouted. 'My wife done teach you fine.'

'Yes, yes,' roared the Fon over the top of Jacquie's head. 'No foine dance dis. Your wife na good wife for me.'

Eventually, after half an hour's dancing, they returned to their chairs, hot and exhausted. The Fon took a large gulp of neat gin to restore himself, and then leaned across to me.

'Dis your wife na foine,' he said in a hoarse whisper, presumably thinking that praise might turn Jacquie's head. 'She dance foine. She done teach me foine. I go give her mimbo . . . special mimbo I go give her.'

I turned to Jacquie who, unaware of her fate, was sitting fanning herself.

'You've certainly made a hit with our host,' I said.

'He's a dear old boy,' said Jacquie, 'and he dances awfully well . . . did you see how he picked up that samba in next to no time?'

'Yes,' I said, 'and he was so delighted with your teaching that he's going to reward you.'

Jacquie looked at me suspiciously. 'How's he going to reward me?' she asked.

'You're now going to receive a calabash of special mimbo . . . palm wine.'

'Oh God, and I can't stand the stuff,' said Jacquie in horror.

'Never mind. Take a glassful, taste it, tell him it's the finest you've ever had, and then ask if he will allow you to share it with his wives.'

Five calabashes were brought, the neck of each plugged with green leaves, and the Fon solemnly tasted them all before making up his mind which was the best vintage. Then a glass was filled and passed to Jacquie. Summoning up all her social graces she took a mouthful, rolled it round her mouth, swallowed and allowed a look of intense satisfaction to appear on her face.

'This is very fine mimbo,' she proclaimed in delighted astonishment, with the air of one who has just been presented with a glass of Napoleon brandy. The Fon beamed. Jacquie took another sip, as he watched her closely. An even more delighted expression appeared on her face.

'This is the best mimbo I've ever tasted,' said Jacquie.

'Ha! Good!' said the Fon, with pleasure. 'Dis na foine mimbo. Na fresh one.'

'Will you let your wives drink with me?' asked Jacquie.

'Yes, yes,' said the Fon with a lordly wave of his hand, and so the wives shuffled forward, grinning shyly, and Jacquie hastily poured the remains of the mimbo into their pink palms.

At this point, the level of the gin bottle having fallen alarmingly, I suddenly glanced at my watch and saw, with horror, that in two and a half hours it would be dawn. So, pleading heavy work on the morrow, I broke up the party. The Fon insisted on accompanying us to the foot of the steps that led up to the Rest House, preceded by the band. Here he embraced us fondly.

'Good night, my friend,' he said, shaking my hand.

'Good night,' I replied. 'Thank you. You done give us happy time.'

'Yes,' said Jacquie, 'thank you very much.'

'Wah!' said the Fon, patting her on the head, 'we done dance foine. You be good wife for me, eh?'

We watched him as he wended his way across the great courtyard, tall and graceful in his robes, the boy trotting beside him carrying the lamp that cast a pool of golden light about him. They disappeared into the tangle of huts, and the twittering of the flutes and the bang of the drums became fainter and died away, until all we could hear was the calls of crickets and tree frogs and the faint honking cries of the fruit bats. Somewhere in the distance the first cock crowed, huskily and sleepily, as we crept under our mosquito nets.

MAIL BY HAND

My good friend,

Good morning to you all.

Your note to me received and contents well understood.

I am a beat relief from that cough but not much.

I agree for you to hire my landrover as from today on weekly payments. I will also want to bring to your notice that the landrover will be under your charge as from today, but any time I am called for a meeting at Ndop, Bemenda or elsewhere, or any urgent matter, I shall inform you to allow me the motor for the day.

I want to remind you of the last trip which you hired the landrover and settlement had not yet been made.

Your good friend,
Fon of Bafut

CHAPTER FOUR

BEEF IN BOXES

As soon as Bob and Sophie had joined us in Bafut we set
about the task of organizing our already large and ever-
growing collection. The great, shady verandah that ran round
the upstairs rooms of the Fon's Rest House was divided into
three: one section for reptiles, one for birds and one for
mammals. Thus each of us had a particular section to look
after and whoever finished first lent a hand with somebody
else's group. First thing in the morning we would all wander
to and fro along the verandah in our pyjamas carefully looking
at each animal to make sure it was all right. It is only by this
day-to-day routine of careful watching that you can get to
know your animals so well that you detect the slightest sign
of illness, when to anyone else the animal would appear to be
perfectly healthy and normal. Then we cleaned and fed all the
delicate animals that could not wait (such as the sunbirds who
had to have their nectar as soon as it was light, and the baby
creatures that needed their early morning bottles) and then we

paused for breakfast. It was during mealtime that we compared notes on our charges. This mealtime conversation would have put any normal mortal off his food, for it was mainly concerned with the bowel movements of our creatures; with wild animals, diarrhoea or constipation is often a good indication as to whether you are feeding it correctly, and it can also be the first (and sometimes the only) symptom of an illness.

On any collecting trip acquiring the animals is, as a rule, the simplest part of the job. As soon as the local people discover that you are willing to buy live wild creatures the stuff comes pouring in; ninety per cent is, of course, the commoner species, but they do bring an occasional rarity. If you want the really rare stuff you generally have to go out and find it yourself, but while you are devoting your time to this you can be sure that all the common local fauna will be brought in to you. So one might almost say that getting the animals is easy: the really hard part is keeping them once you have got them.

The chief difficulty you have to contend with when you have got a newly caught animal is not so much the shock it might be suffering from capture, but the fact that the capture forces it to exist in close proximity to a creature it regards as an enemy of the worst possible sort: yourself. On many occasions an animal may take to captivity beautifully, but can never reconcile itself to the intimate terms on which it has to exist with man. This is the first great barrier to break down and you can only do it by patience and kindness. For month after month an animal may snap and snarl at you every time you approach its cage, until you begin to despair of ever making a favourable impression on it. Then, one day, sometimes without any preliminary warning, it will trot forward and take food from your hand, or allow you to tickle it behind the ears. At such moments you feel that all the waiting in the world was justified.

Feeding, of course, is one of your main problems. Not only must you have a fairly extensive knowledge of what each species eats in the wild state, but you have to work out a suitable substitute if the natural food is unavailable, and then teach your specimen to eat it. You also have to cater for their individual likes and dislikes, which vary enormously. I have known a rodent which, refusing all normal rodent food – such as fruit, bread, vegetables – live for three days on an exclusive diet of spaghetti. I have had a group of five monkeys, of the same age and species, who displayed the most weird idiosyncrasies. Out of the five, two had a passion for hard-boiled eggs, while the other three were frightened of the strange white shapes and would not touch them, actually screaming in fear if you introduced such a fearsome object as a hard-boiled egg into their cage. These five monkeys all adored orange but, whereas four would carefully peel their fruit and throw away the skin, the fifth would peel his orange equally carefully and then throw away the orange and eat the peel. When you have a collection of several hundred creatures all displaying such curious characteristics you are sometimes nearly driven mad in your efforts to satisfy their desires, and so keep them healthy and happy.

But of all the irritating and frustrating tasks that you have to undertake during a collecting trip, the hand-rearing of baby animals is undoubtedly the worst. To begin with, they are generally stupid over taking a bottle and there is nothing quite so unattractive as struggling with a baby animal in a sea of lukewarm milk. Secondly, they have to be kept warm, especially at night, and this means (unless you take them to bed with you, which is often the answer) you have to get up several times during the night to replenish hot-water bottles. After a hard day's work, to drag yourself out of bed at three in the morning to fill hot-water bottles is an occupation that soon loses its charm. Thirdly, all baby animals have extremely delicate stomachs and you must watch them like a hawk to make sure that the milk you are giving them is not too rich or too weak; if too rich, they can develop intestinal troubles which may lead to nephritis, which will probably kill them, and if too weak, it can lead to loss of weight and condition, which leaves the animal open to all sorts of fatal complaints.

Contrary to my gloomy prognostications, the baby black-eared squirrel, Squill-lill Small (Small to her friends) proved an exemplary baby. During the day she lay twitching in a bed of cotton-wool balanced on a hot-water bottle in the bottom of a deep biscuit-tin; at night the tin was placed by our beds under the rays of a Tilley infra-red heater. Almost immediately we were made aware of the fact that Small had a will of her own. For such a tiny animal she could produce an extraordinary volume of noise, her cry being a loud and rapid series of 'chucks' that sounded like a cheap alarm clock going off. Within the first twenty-four hours she had learnt when to expect her feeds and if we were as much as five minutes late she would trill and chuck incessantly until we arrived with the food. Then came the day when Small's eyes opened for the first time and she could take a look at her foster parents and the world in general. This, however, presented a new problem. We happened that day to be a bit late with her food. We had rather dawdled over our own lunch, deep in a discussion about some problem or other, and we had, I regret to say, forgotten all about Small. Suddenly I heard a faint scuffling behind me and, turning round, I saw Small squatting in the doorway of the dining-room looking, to say the least, extremely indignant. As soon as she saw us she went off like an alarm clock and hurrying across the floor hauled herself, panting, up Jacquie's chair and then leapt to her shoulder, where she sat flicking her tail up and down and shouting indignantly into Jacquie's ear. Now this, for a baby squirrel, was quite a feat. To begin with, as I say, her eyes had only just opened. Yet she had succeeded in climbing out of her tin and finding her way out of our bedroom (piled high with camera equipment and film); she had made her way down the full length of the verandah, running the gauntlet of any number of cages filled with potentially dangerous beasts, and eventually located us (presumably by sound) in the dining-room which was at the extreme end of the verandah. She had covered seventy yards over unknown territory, through innumerable dangers, in order to tell us she was hungry. Needless to say, she got her due of praise and what was more important from her point of view, she got her lunch.

As soon as Small's eyes opened she grew rapidly and soon developed into one of the loveliest squirrels I have ever seen. Her orange head and neat, black-rimmed ears nicely set off her large dark eyes, and her fat body developed a rich moss green tinge against which the two lines of white spots that decorated her sides stood out like cats'-eyes on a dark road. But her tail was her best feature. Long and thick, green above and vivid orange below, it was a beautiful sight. She liked to sit with it curved over her back, the tip actually hanging over her nose, and then she would flick it gently in an undulating movement so that the whole thing looked like a candle flame in a draught.

Even when she was quite grown-up, Small slept in her biscuit-tin by my bed. She awoke early in the morning and, uttering her loud cry, she leaped from the tin on to one of our beds and crawled under the bed-clothes with us. Having spent ten minutes or so investigating our semi-comatose bodies, she jumped to the floor and went to explore the verandah. From these expeditions she would frequently return with some treasure she had found (such as a bit of rotten banana, or a dry leaf, or a bougainvillaea flower) and store it somewhere in our beds, getting most indignant if we hurled the offering out on to the floor. This continued for some months, until the day when I decided that Small would have to occupy a cage like the rest of the animals; I awoke one morning in excruciating agony to find her trying to stuff a peanut into my ear. Having found such a delicacy on the verandah she obviously thought that simply to cache it in my bed was not safe enough, but my ear provided an ideal hiding-place.

Bug-eyes, the needle-clawed lemur we had captured near

Eshobi, was another baby, although she was fully weaned when we found her. She had become tame in a short space of time and very rapidly became one of our favourites. For her size she had enormous hands and feet, with long, attenuated fingers, and to see her dancing around her cage on her hind legs, her immense hands held up as though in horror, her eyes almost popping out of her head, as she pursued a moth or butterfly we had introduced, was a delightfully comic spectacle. Once she had caught it she sat there with it clasped tightly in her pink hand and regarded it with a wild, wide-eyed stare, as if amazed that such a creature should suddenly appear in the palm of her hand. Then she stuffed it into her mouth and continued to sit with what appeared to be a fluttering moustache of butterfly wing decorating her face, over which her huge eyes peered in astonishment.

It was Bug-eyes who first showed me an extraordinary habit that bushbabies have, a habit which to my shame I had never noticed before, in spite of the fact that I had kept innumerable bushbabies. I was watching her one morning when she had popped out of her nesting box for a feed of mealworms and a quick wash and brush up. She had, as I said before, large ears which were as delicate as flower petals. They were so fine that they were almost transparent and, presumably to prevent them from becoming torn or damaged in the wild state, she had the power of folding them back against the sides of her head like the furled sails of a yacht. Her ears were terribly important to her as you could tell by watching her. The slightest sound, however faint, would be picked up and her ears would twitch and turn towards it like radar. Now I had always noticed that she spent a lot of time cleaning and rubbing her ears with her hands, but on this particular morning I watched the whole process from start to finish and was considerably startled by what I saw. She began by sitting on a branch, staring dreamily into space while she daintily cleaned her tail, parting the hair carefully and making sure there were no snags or tangles,

reminding me of a little girl plaiting her hair. Then she put one of her outsize, puppet-like hands beneath her and deposited in the palm a drop of urine. With an air of concentration, she rubbed her hands together and proceeded to anoint her ears with the urine, rather after the manner of a man rubbing brilliantine into his hair. Then she got another drop of urine and rubbed it carefully over the soles of her feet and the palms of her hands, while I sat and watched her in amazement.

I watched her do this three days in succession before I was satisfied that I was not imagining things, for it seemed to me to be one of the weirdest animal habits I had ever encountered. I can only conclude that the reason for it was this: unless the skin of the ears, so extremely delicate and thin, were kept moistened it must inevitably get dry and perhaps crack, which would have been fatal for an animal that relied so much on hearing. The same would apply to the delicate skin on the soles of her feet and hands, but here the urine would also provide an additional advantage. The soles of feet and hands were slightly cupped, so that as the creature leapt from bough to bough the hands and feet acted almost like the suckers on the toes of a tree-frog. Now, moistened with urine, these 'suckers' became twice as efficient. When, later on in the trip, we obtained a great number of Demidoff's bushbabies (the smallest of the tribe, each being the size of a large mouse) I noticed that they all had the same habit.

This is, to my mind, the best part of a collecting trip, the close daily contact with the animals that allows you to observe, learn and record. Every day, and almost at every moment of the day, something new and interesting was happening somewhere in the collection. The following diary entries show fairly well how each day bristled with new tasks and interesting observations:

February 14: Two patas monkeys brought in; both had severe infestation of jiggers in toes and fingers. Had to lance them, extract jiggers and as precaution against infection injected penicillin. Baby civet did her first adult 'display', making the mane of hair on her back stand up when I approached her cage suddenly. She accompanied this action with several loud sniffs, much deeper and more penetrating than her normal sniffing round food. Large brow-leaf toad brought in with extraordinary eye trouble. What appears to be a large malignant growth, situated behind the eyeball, had blinded the creature and then

grown outwards, so that the toad looked as though it was wearing a large balloon over one eye. It did not appear to be suffering so am not attempting to remove the growth. So much for animals being happy and carefree in the wild state.

February 20: At last, after much trial and error, Bob has discovered what the hairy frogs eat: snails. We had previously tried young mice and rats, baby birds, eggs, beetles and their larvae, locusts, all without success. Snails they devour avidly, so we have high hopes of getting the frogs back alive. Have had an outbreak of what appears to be nephritis among the Demidoff's bushbabies. Two discovered this morning drenched in urine as though they had been dipped. Have weakened the milk they get; it may be too strong. Also organized more insect food for them. The five baby Demidoff's are still thriving on their Complan milk, which is curious as this is incredibly rich, and if ordinary dried milk affects the adults one would have thought Complan would have had a similar effect on the babies.

March 16: Two nice cobras brought in, one about six feet long and the other about two feet. Both fed straight away. Best item today was female pigmy mongoose and two babies. The babies are still blind and an extraordinary pale fawn in contrast to the dark brown mother. Have removed babies to hand-rear them as felt sure female would either neglect or kill them if they were put with her.

March 17: Young pigmy mongooses flatly refuse to feed from bottle or from fountain-pen filler. In view of this (since their chances seemed slim) put them into cage with female. To my surprise she has accepted them and is suckling them well. Most unusual. Had two broken leg jobs today: Woodford's owl which had been caught in a gin-trap and a young hawk with a greenstick fracture. I don't think the owl will regain use of leg for all the ligaments appear to be torn, and the bone badly splintered. Hawk's leg should be O.K. as it's a young bird. Both are feeding well. Demidoff's make a faint mewing hiss when disturbed at night, the only sound I have heard them make apart from their bat-like twittering when fighting. Clawed toads have started to call at night: very faint 'peep-peep' noise, rather like someone flicking the edge of a glass gently with finger-nail.

April 2: Young male chimp, about two years old, brought in today. Was in a terrible mess. Had been caught in one of the wire noose-traps they use for antelopes, and had damaged its left hand and arm. The palm of the hand and the wrist were split right open and badly infected with gangrene. The animal was very weak, not being able to sit up, and the colour of the skin was a curious yellowish grey. Attended to wound and injected penicillin. Drove it in to Bemenda for the Dept. of Agriculture's vet to have a look at, as did not like skin colour or curious lethargy in spite of stimulants. He took blood test and diagnosed sleeping-sickness. Have done all we can but the animal appears to be sinking fast. He seems pathetically grateful for anything you do for him.

April 3: Chimp died. They are a 'protected' animal and yet up here, as in other parts of the Cameroons, they are killed and eaten regularly. Big rhinoceros viper fed for first time: small rat. One of the green forest squirrels appears to be developing a bald patch on his back: presume lack of vitamins so am increasing his Abidec. As we now get good supply of weaver-birds' eggs each day all the squirrels are getting them, in addition to their normal diet. The brush-tail porcupines, when disturbed at night beat rapid tattoo with their hind-feet (like a wild rabbit) then swing their backside round to face danger and rustle bunch of quills on end of tail, producing a sound reminiscent of rattle-snake.

April 5: Have found simple, rapid way of sexing pottos. Nice young male brought in today. Although external genitalia in both sexes are remarkably similar to a superficial glance, have discovered that simplest way is to smell them. The testicles of the male give out a faint, sweet odour, like pear drops, when the animal is handled.

We were not the only ones interested in the animals. Many of the local people had never seen some of the creatures we had acquired, and many called and asked for permission to look round the collection. One day the Headmaster of the local Mission School called and asked if he could bring his entire school of two-hundred-odd boys to see the collection. I was glad to agree to this, for I feel that if you can, by showing live animals, arouse people's interest in their local fauna and its preservation you are doing something worthwhile. So, on the appointed date, the boys came marching down the road in a double column, shepherded by five masters. In the road below the Rest House the boys were divided up into groups of twenty and then brought up in turn by a master. Jacquie, Sophie, Bob and I took up stations at various points in the collection to answer any queries. The boys behaved in a model fashion; there was no pushing or shoving, no skylarking. They wended their way from cage to cage, absorbed and fascinated, uttering amazed cries of 'Wah!' at each new wonder and clicking their fingers in delight. Finally, when the last group had been led round, the Headmaster grouped all the boys at the bottom of the steps and then turned to me, beaming.

'Sir,' he said, 'we are very grateful to you for allowing us to see your zoological collections. May I ask if you would be kind enough to answer some of the boys' questions?'

'Yes, with pleasure,' I said, taking up my stand on the steps above the crowd.

'Boys,' roared the Head, 'Mr Durrell has kindly say that he will answer any questions. Now who has a question?'

The sea of black faces below me screwed themselves up in thought, tongues protruded, toes wiggled in the dust. Then, slowly at first, but with increasing speed as they lost their embarrassment, they shot questions at me, all of which were extremely intelligent and sensible. There was, I noticed, one small boy in the front of the crowd who had, throughout the proceedings, fixed me with a basilisk eye. His brow was furrowed with concentration, and he stood stiffly at attention. At last, when the supply of questions started to peter out, he suddenly summoned up all his courage, and shot his hand up.

'Yes, Uano, what is your question?' asked the Head, smiling down fondly at the boy.

The boy took a deep breath and then fired his question at me rapidly. 'Please, sah, can Mr Durrell tell us why he take so many photographs of the Fon's wives?'

The smile vanished from the Head's face and he threw me a look of chagrin.

'That is not a zoological question, Uano,' he pointed out severely.

'But please, sah, why?' repeated the child stubbornly.

The Head scowled ferociously. 'That is *not* a zoological question,' he thundered. 'Mr Durrell only said he would answer zoological questions. The matter of the Fon's wives is not zoological.'

'Well, loosely speaking it could be called biological, Headmaster, couldn't it?' I asked, coming to the lad's rescue.

'But, sir, they shouldn't ask you questions like that,' said the Head, mopping his face.

'Well, I don't mind answering. The reason is that, in my country, everyone is very interested to know how people in other parts of the world live and what they look like. I can tell them, of course, but it's not the same as if they see a photograph. With a photograph they know exactly what everything is like.'

'There . . .' said the Headmaster, running a finger round the inside of his collar. 'There, Mr Durrell has answered your question. Now, he is a very busy man so there is no more time for further questions. Kindly get into line.'

The boys formed themselves once more into two orderly lines, while the Headmaster shook my hand and earnestly assured me that they were all most grateful. Then he turned once more to the boys.

'Now, to show our appreciation to Mr Durrell I want three hearty cheers.'

Two hundred young lungs boomed out the hearty cheers. Then the boys at the head of the line produced from bags they were carrying several bamboo flutes and two small drums. The Headmaster waved his hand and they started to walk off down the road, led by the school band playing, of all things, 'Men of Harlech'. The Head followed them mopping his face, and the dark looks he kept darting at young Uano's back did not augur well for the boy's prospects when he got back to the classroom.

That evening the Fon came over for a drink and, after we had shown him the new additions to the collection, we sat on the verandah and I told him about Uano's zoological question. The Fon laughed and laughed, particularly at the embarrassment of the Headmaster. 'Why you never tell um,' he inquired, wiping his eyes, 'why you never tell um dat you take dis photo of dis ma wife for show all Europeans for your country dat Bafut women be beautiful?'

'Dis boy na picken,' I said solemnly. 'I think sometime he be too small to understand dis woman palaver.'

'Na true, na true,' said the Fon, chuckling, ''e be picken. 'E catch lucky, 'e no get women for humbug him.'

'They tell me, my friend,' I said, trying to steer the conversation away from the pros and cons of married life, 'they tell me tomorrow you go for N'dop. Na so?'

'Na so,' said the Fon, 'I go for two days, for Court. I go come back for morning time tomorrow tomorrow.'

'Well,' I said, raising my glass, 'safe journey, my friend.'

The following morning, clad in splendid yellow and black robes and wearing a curious hat, heavily embroidered, with long, drooping ear flaps, the Fon took his seat in the front of his new Land-Rover. Into the back went the necessities of travel: three bottles of Scotch, his favourite wife and three council members. He waved vigorously to us until the vehicle rounded the corner and was lost from sight.

That evening, having finished the last chores of the day, I went out on to the front verandah for a breath of air. In the great courtyard below I noticed large numbers of the Fon's children assembling. Curiously I watched them. They grouped themselves in a huge circle in the centre of the compound and, after much discussion and argument, they started to sing and clap their hands rhythmically, accompanied by a seven-year-old who stood in the centre of the circle beating a drum. Standing like this they lifted up their young voices and sang some of the most beautiful and haunting of the Bafut songs. This, I could tell, was not just an ordinary gathering of children; they had assembled there for some definite purpose, but what they were celebrating (unless it was their father's departure) I could not think. I stood there watching them for a long time and then John, our houseboy, appeared at my elbow in his unnervingly silent way.

'Dinner ready, sah,' he said.

'Thank you, John. Tell me, why all dis picken sing for the Fon's compound?'

John smiled shyly. 'Because de Fon done go for N'dop, sah.'

'Yes, but why they sing?'

'If the Fon no be here, sah, each night dis picken must for sing inside de Fon's compound. So dey keep dis his compound warm.'

This, I thought, was a delightful idea. I peered down at the circle of children, singing lustily in the gloomy wastes of the great courtyard, to keep their father's compound warm.

'Why they never dance?' I asked.

'Dey never get light, sah.'

'Take them the pressure light from the bedroom. Tell them I send it so that I can help keep the Fon's compound warm.'

'Yes, sah,' said John. He hurried off to fetch the light and presently I saw it cast a golden pool round the circle of children. There was a pause in the singing, while John delivered my message, and then came a series of delighted shrieks and echoing up to me the shrill voices crying, 'Tank you, Masa, tank you.'

As we sat down to dinner the children were singing like larks, and stamping and weaving their way round the lamp, their shadows long and attenuated, thrown half-way across the courtyard by the softly hissing lamp in their midst.

My good friend,

Would you like to come and have a drink with us this evening at eight o'clock?

Your friend,
Gerald Durrell

My good friend,

Expect me a 7.30 p.m. Thanks.

Your good friend,
Fon of Bafut

CHAPTER FIVE

FILM STAR BEEF

THERE are several different ways of making an animal film, and probably one of the best methods is to employ a team of cameramen who spend about two years in some tropical part of the world filming the animals in their natural state. Unfortunately this method is expensive, and unless you have the time and the resources of Hollywood behind you it is out of the question.

For someone like myself, with only a limited amount of time and money to spend in a country, the only way to film animals is under controlled conditions. The difficulties of trying to film wild animals in a tropical forest are enough to make even the most ardent photographer grow pale. To begin with you hardly ever see a wild animal and, when you do, it is generally only a momentary glimpse as it scuttles off into the undergrowth. To be in the right spot at the right time with your camera set up, your exposure correct and an animal in front of you in a suitable setting, engaged in some interesting and filmable action, would be almost a miracle. So, the only way round this is to catch your animal first and establish it in captivity. Once it has lost some of its fear of human beings you can begin work. Inside a huge netting 'room' you create a scene which is as much like the animal's natural habitat as possible, and yet which is – photographically speaking – suitable. That is to say, it must not have too many holes in which a shy creature can hide, your undergrowth must not be so thick that you get awkward patches of shade, and so on. Then you introduce your animal to the set, and allow it time to settle down, which may be anything from an hour to a couple of days.

It is essential, of course, to have a good knowledge of the animal's habits, and to know how it will react under certain circumstances. For example, a hungry pouched rat, if released in an appropriate setting and finding a lavish selection of forest fruits on the ground, will promptly proceed to stuff as many of them into his immense cheek pouches as they will hold, so that in the end he looks as though he is suffering from a particularly virulent attack of mumps. If you don't want to end up with nothing more exciting than a series of pictures of some creature wandering aimlessly to and fro amid bushes and grass, you must provide the circumstances which will allow it to display some interesting habit or action. However, even when you have reached this stage you still require two other things: patience and luck. An animal – even a tame one – cannot be told what to do like a human actor. Sometimes a creature which has performed a certain action day after day for weeks will, when faced with a camera, develop an acute attack of stage fright, and refuse to perform. When you have spent hours in the hot sun getting everything ready, to be treated to this sort of display of temperament makes you feel positively homicidal.

A prize example of the difficulties of animal photography

was, I think, the day we attempted to photograph the water chevrotain. These delightful little antelopes are about the size of a fox-terrier, with a rich chestnut coat handsomely marked with streaks and spots of white. Small and dainty, the water chevrotain is extremely photogenic. There are several interesting points about the chevrotain, one of which is its adaptation to a semi-aquatic life in the wild state. It spends most of its time wading and swimming in streams in the forest and can even swim for considerable distances under water. The second curious thing is that it has a passion for snails and beetles, and such carnivorous habits in an antelope are most unusual. The third notable characteristic is its extraordinary placidity and tameness: I have known a chevrotain, an hour after capture, take food from my hand and allow me to tickle its ears, for all the world as if it had been born in captivity.

Our water chevrotain was no exception; she was ridiculously tame, adored having her head and tummy scratched and would engulf, with every sign of satisfaction, any quantity of snails and beetles you cared to provide. Apart from this she spent her spare time trying to bathe in her water bowl, into which she could just jam – with considerable effort – the extreme rear end of her body.

So, to display her carnivorous and aquatic habits, I designed a set embracing a section of river bank. The undergrowth was carefully placed so that it would show off her perfect adaptive coloration to the best advantage. One morning, when the sky was free from cloud and the sun was in the right place, we carried the chevrotain cage out to the set and prepared to release her.

'The only thing I'm afraid of,' I said to Jacquie, 'is that I'm not going to get sufficient movement out of her. You know how quiet she is . . . she'll probably walk into the middle of the set and refuse to move.'

'Well, if we offer her a snail or something from the other side I should think she'll walk across,' said Jacquie.

'As long as she doesn't just stand there, like a cow in a field. I want to get *some* movement out of her,' I said.

I got considerably more movement out of her than I anticipated. The moment the slide of her cage was lifted she stepped out daintily and paused with one slender hoof raised. I started the camera and awaited her next move. Her next move was somewhat unexpected. She shot across my carefully prepared set like a rocket, went right through the netting wall as if it had not been there and disappeared into the undergrowth in the middle distance before any of us could make a move to stop her. Our reactions were slow, because this was the last thing we had expected, but as I saw my precious chevrotain disappearing from view I uttered such a wail of anguish that everyone, including Phillip the cook, dropped whatever they were doing and assembled on the scene like magic.

'Water beef done run,' I yelled. 'I go give ten shillings to the man who go catch um.'

The effect of this lavish offer was immediate. A wedge of

Africans descended on to the patch of undergrowth into which
the antelope had disappeared, like a swarm of hungry locusts.
Within five minutes Phillip, uttering a roar of triumph like a
sergeant-major, emerged from the bushes clutching to his
bosom the kicking, struggling antelope. When we replaced her
in her cage she stood quite quietly, gazing at us with limpid
eyes as if astonished at all the fuss. She licked my hand in a
friendly fashion, and when tickled behind the ears went off
into her usual trance-like state, with half-closed eyes. We spent
the rest of the day trying to film the wretched creature. She
behaved beautifully in her box, splashing in a bowl of water to
show how aquatic she was, eating beetles and snails to show
how carnivorous she was, but the moment she was released
into the film set she fled towards the horizon as if she had a
brace of leopards on her tail. At the end of the day, hot and
exhausted, I had exposed fifty feet of film, all of which showed
her standing stock still outside her box, preparatory to dashing
away. Sadly we carried her cage back to the Rest House, while
she lay placidly on her banana-leaf bed and munched beetles.
It was the last time we tried to photograph the water chevrotain.

Another creature that caused me untold anguish in the
photographic field was a young Woodford's owl called, with
singular lack of originality, Woody. Woodfords are very
lovely owls, with a rich chocolate plumage splashed and
blotched with white, and possessing what must be the most
beautiful eyes in the whole of the owl family. They are large,
dark and liquid, with heavy lids of a delicate pinky-mauve.
These they raise and lower over their eyes in what seems to
be slow motion, like an ancient film actress considering whether
to make a comeback. This seductive fluttering of eyelids is
accompanied by loud clickings of the beak-like castanets. When
excited the eyelid fluttering becomes very pronounced and the
birds sway from side to side on the perch, as if about to start
a hula-hula, and then they suddenly spread their wings and

stand there clicking their beaks at you, looking like a tombstone angel of the more fiercely religious variety. Woody would perform all these actions perfectly inside his cage and would, moreover, perform them to order when shown a succulent tit-bit like a small mouse. I felt sure that, if he was provided with a suitable background, I could get his display on film with the minimum of trouble.

So, in the netting room I used for bird photography I set to and created what looked like a forest tree, heavily overgrown with creepers and other parasites, using green leaves and a blue sky as background. Then I carried Woody out and placed him on the branch in the midst of this wealth of foliage. The action I wanted him to perform was a simple and natural one not calculated to tax even the brain of an owl. With a little co-operation on his part the whole thing could have been over in ten minutes. He sat on the branch regarding us with wide-eyed horror, while I took up my position behind the camera. Just as I pressed the button he blinked his eyes once, very rapidly, and then, as if overcome with disgust at our appearance, he very firmly turned his back on us. Trying to remember that patience was the first requisite of an animal photographer, I wiped the sweat from my eyes, walked up to the branch, turned him round and walked back to the camera. By the time I had reached it Woody once more had his back towards us. I thought that maybe the light was too strong, so several members of the staff were sent to cut branches and these were rigged up so that the bird was sheltered from the direct rays of the sun. But still he persisted in keeping his back to us. It was obvious that, if I wanted to photograph him. I would have to rearrange my set so that it faced the opposite way. After considerable labour about a ton of undergrowth was carefully shifted and rearranged so that Woody was now facing the way he obviously preferred.

During this labour, while we sweated with massive branches and coils of creepers, he sat there regarding us in surprise. He

generously allowed me to get the camera set up in the right
position (a complicated job, for I was now shooting almost
directly into the sun) and then he calmly turned his back on it.
I could have strangled him. By this time ominous black clouds
were rolling up, preparatory to obscuring the sun, and so
further attempts at photography were impossible. I packed
up the camera and then walked to the branch, murder in my
heart, to collect my star. As I approached he turned round,
clicked his beak delightedly, executed a rapid hula-hula and
then spread his wings and bowed to me, with the mock-shy
air of an actor taking his seventeenth curtain call.

Of course not all our stars caused us trouble. In fact, one of
the best sequences I managed to get on film was accomplished
with the minimum of fuss and in record time. And yet, on the
face of it, one would have thought that it was a much more
difficult object to achieve than getting an owl to spread his
wings. Simply, I wanted to get some shots of an egg-eating
snake robbing a nest. Egg-eating snakes measure about two
feet in length and are very slender. Coloured a pinkish-brown,
mottled with darker markings, they have strange, protuberant
eyes of a pale silvery colour with fine vertical pupils like a
cat's. The curious point about them is that three inches from
the throat (internally, of course) the vertebrae protrude,
hanging down like stalactites. The reptile engulfs an egg, whole,
and this passes down its body until it lies directly under these
vertebrae. Then the snake contracts its muscles and the spikes
penetrate the egg and break it; the yolk and white are absorbed
and the broken shell, now a flattened pellet, is regurgitated.
The whole process is quite extraordinary and had never, as far
as I knew, been recorded on film.

We had, at that time, six egg-eating snakes, all of which
were, to my delight, identical in size and coloration. The local
children did a brisk trade in bringing us weaver-birds' eggs to
feed this troupe of reptiles, for they seemed capable of eating
any number we cared to put in their cage. In fact, the mere

introduction of an egg into the cage changed them from a somnolent pile of snakes to a writhing bundle, each endeavouring to get at the egg first. But, although they behaved so beautifully in the cage, after my experiences with Woody and the water chevrotain, I was inclined to be a bit pessimistic. However, I created a suitable set (a flowering bush in the branches of which was placed a small nest) and collected a dozen small blue eggs as props. Then the snakes were kept without their normal quota of eggs for three days, to make sure they all had good appetites. This, incidentally, did not hurt them at all, for all snakes can endure considerable fasts, which with some of the bigger constrictors run into months or years. However, when my stars had got what I hoped was a good edge to their appetites, we started work.

The snakes' cage was carried out to the film set, five lovely blue eggs were placed in the nest and then one of the reptiles was placed gently in the branches of the bush, just above the nest. I started the camera and waited.

The snake lay flaccidly across the branches seeming a little dazed by the sunlight after the cool dimness of its box. In a moment its tongue started to flicker in and out, and it turned its head from side to side in an interested manner. Then with smooth fluidity it started to trickle through the branches towards the nest. Slowly it drew closer and closer, and when it reached the rim of the nest, it peered over the edge and down at the eggs with its fierce silvery eyes. Its tongue flicked again as if it were smelling the eggs and it nosed them gently like a dog with a pile of biscuits. Then it pulled itself a little farther into the nest, turned its head sideways, opened its mouth wide and started to engulf one of the eggs. All snakes have a jaw so constructed that they can dislocate the hinge, which enables them to swallow a prey that, at first sight, looks too big to pass through their mouths. The egg-eater was no exception and he neatly dislocated his jaws and the skin of his throat stretched until each scale stood out individually and you could see the blue of the egg shining through the fine, taut skin as the egg was forced slowly down his throat. When the egg was about an inch down his body he paused for a moment's meditation and then swung himself out of the nest and into the branches. Here, as he made his way along, he rubbed the great swelling in his body that the egg had created against the branches so that the egg was forced farther and farther down.

Elated with this success we returned the snake to his box so that he could digest his meal in comfort, and I shifted the camera's position and put on my big lenses for close-up work. We put another egg into the nest to replace the one taken, and then got out another egg-eater. This was the beauty of having all the snakes of the same size and coloration: as the first snake would not look at another egg until he had digested the first, he could not be used in the close-up shots. But the new one was identical and as hungry as a hunter, and so without any trouble whatsoever I got all the close-up shots I needed as he glided rapidly down to the nest and took an egg. I did the whole thing all over again with two other snakes and on the finished film these four separate sequences were intercut and no one, seeing the finished product, could tell that they were seeing four different snakes.

All the Bafutians, including the Fon, were fascinated by our filming activities, since not long before they had seen their very first cinema. A mobile ciné van had come out to Bafut and shown them a colour film of the Coronation and they had been terribly thrilled with it. In fact it was still a subject of grave discussion when we were there, nearly a year and a half later. Thinking that the Fon and his council would be interested to learn more about filming, I invited them to come across one morning and attend a filming session and they accepted with delight.

'What are you going to film?' asked Jacquie.

'Well, it doesn't really matter, so long as it's innocuous,' I said.

'Why innocuous?' asked Sophie.

'I don't want to take any risks. . . . If I got the Fon bitten by something I would hardly be *persona grata*, would I?'

'Good God, no, that would never do,' said Bob. 'What sort of thing did you have in mind?'

'Well, I want to get some shots of those pouched rats, so we might as well use them. They can't hurt a fly.'

So the following morning we got everything ready. The film set, representing a bit of forest floor, had been constructed on a Dexion stand, one of our specially made nylon tarpaulins had been erected nearby, under which the Fon and his court could sit, and beneath it were placed a table of drinks and some chairs. Then we sent a message over to the Fon that we were ready for him.

We watched him and his council approaching across the great courtyard and they were a wonderful spectacle. First came the Fon, in handsome blue and white robes, his favourite wife trotting along beside him, shading him from the sun with an enormous orange and red umbrella. Behind him walked the council members in their fluttering robes of green, red, orange, scarlet, white and yellow. Around this phalanx of colour some forty-odd of the Fon's children skipped and scuttled about like little black beetles round a huge, multi-coloured caterpillar. Slowly the procession made its way round the Rest House and arrived at our improvised film studio.

'Morning, my friend,' called the Fon, grinning. 'We done come for see dis cinema.'

'Welcome, my friend,' I replied. 'You like first we go have drink together?'

'Wah! Yes, I like,' said the Fon, lowering himself cautiously into one of our camp chairs.

I poured out the drinks, and as we sipped them I explained the mysteries of ciné photography to the Fon, showing him how the camera worked, what the film itself looked like and explaining how each little picture was of a separate movement.

'Dis filum you take, when we go see um?' asked the Fon, when he had mastered the basic principles of photography.

'I have to take um for my country before it get ready,' I said sadly, 'so I no fit show you until I go come back for the Cameroons.'

'Ah, good,' said the Fon, 'so when you go come back for dis ma country we go have happy time and you go show me dis your filum.'

We had another drink to celebrate the thought of my impending return to Bafut.

By this time everything was ready to show the Fon how one set about making a sequence. Sophie, as continuity girl, wear-ing trousers, shirt, sun-glasses and an outsize straw hat, was perched precariously on a small camp-stool, her pad and pencil at the ready to make notes of each shot I took. Near her Jacquie, a battery of still cameras slung round her, was crouched by the side of the recording machine. Near the set, Bob stood in the role of dramatic coach, armed with a twig, and the box in which our stars were squeaking vociferously. I set up the camera, took up my position behind it and gave the signal for action. The Fon and councillors watched silent and absorbed as Bob gently tipped the two pouched rats out on to the set, and then guided them into the right positions with his twig. I started the camera and at the sound of its high-pitched humming a chorus of appreciative 'Ahs' ran through the audience behind me. It was just at that moment that a small boy carrying a calabash wandered into the compound and, oblivious of the crowd, walked up to Bob and held up his offering. I was fully absorbed in peering through the viewfinder of the camera and so I paid little attention to the ensuing conversation that Bob had with the child.

'Na whatee dis?' asked Bob, taking the calabash, which had its neck plugged with green leaves.

'Beef,' said the child succinctly.

Instead of inquiring more closely into the nature of the beef, Bob pulled out the plug of leaves blocking the neck of the calabash. The result surprised not only him but everyone else as well. Six feet of agile and extremely angry green mamba shot out of the calabash like a jack-in-the-box and fell to the ground.

'Mind your feet!' Bob shouted warningly.

I removed my eye from the viewfinder of the camera to be treated to the somewhat disturbing sight of the green mamba sliding determinedly through the legs of the tripod towards me. I leaped upwards and backwards with an airy grace that only a prima ballerina treading heavily on a tin-tack could have emulated. Immediately pandemonium broke loose. The snake slid past me and made for Sophie at considerable speed. Sophie took one look and decided that discretion was the better part of valour. Seizing her pencil, pad and, for some obscure reason, her camp stool too, she ran like a hare towards the massed ranks of the councillors. Unfortunately this was the way the snake wanted to go as well, so he followed hotly on her trail. The councillors took one look at Sophie, apparently leading the snake into their midst, and did not hesitate for a moment.

As one man, they turned and fled. Only the Fon remained, rooted to his chair, so wedged behind the table of drinks that he could not move. 'Get a stick,' I yelled to Bob and ran after the snake. I knew, of course, that the snake would not deliberately attack anyone. It was merely trying to put the greatest possible distance between itself and us. But when you have fifty panic-stricken Africans, all bare-footed, running madly in all directions, accompanied by a frightened and deadly snake, an accident is possible. The scene now, according to Jacquie, was fantastic. The council members were running across the compound, pursued by Sophie, who was pursued by the snake, who was pursued by me, who, in turn, was being pursued by Bob with a stick. The mamba had, to my relief, by-passed the Fon. Since the wave of battle had missed him the Fon sat there and did nothing more constructive than help himself to a quick drink to soothe his shattered nerves.

At last Bob and I managed to corner the mamba against the Rest House steps. Then we held it down with a stick, picked it up and popped it into one of our capacious snake-bags. I returned to the Fon, and found the council members drifting back from various points of the compass to join their monarch. If in any other part of the world you had put to flight a cluster of dignitaries by introducing a snake into their midst, you would have had to suffer endless recriminations, sulks, wounded dignity and other exhausting displays of human nature. But not so with the Africans. The Fon sat in his chair, beaming. The councillors chattered and laughed as they approached, clicking their fingers at the danger that was past, making fun of each other for running so fast, and generally thoroughly enjoying the humorous side of the situation.

'You done hold um, my friend?' asked the Fon, generously pouring me out a large dollop of my own whisky.

'Yes,' I said, taking the drink gratefully, 'we done hold um.'

The Fon leaned across and grinned at me mischievously. 'You see how all dis ma people run?' he asked.

'Yes, they run time no dere,' I agreed.

'They de fear,' explained the Fon.

'Yes. Na bad snake dat.'

'Na true, na true,' agreed the Fon, 'all dis small small man de fear dis snake too much.'

'Yes.'

'I never fear dis snake,' said the Fon. 'All dis ma people dey de run . . . dey de fear too much . . . but I never run.'

'No, my friend, na true . . . you never run.'

'I no de fear dis snake,' said the Fon in case I had missed the point.

'Na true. But dis snake 'e de fear you.'

''E de fear me?' asked the Fon, puzzled.

'Yes, dis snake no fit bite you . . . na bad snake, but he no fit kill Fon of Bafut.'

The Fon laughed uproariously at this piece of blatant flattery, and then, remembering the way his councillors had fled, he laughed again, and the councillors joined him. At length, still reeling with merriment at the incident, they left us and we could hear their chatter and hilarious laughter long after they had disappeared. This is the only occasion when I have known a green mamba to pull off a diplomatic *coup d'état*.

My good friend,

Good morning to you all. I received your note, but sorry my sickness is still going on as it was yesterday.

I was sorry for I failed coming to drink with you, due to the sickness.

I was grateful for the bottle of whiskey and the medicine which you sent to me. I used the medicine yesterday evening and today morning, but no improvement yet. The thing which is giving me trouble is cough, if you can get some medicine for it, kindly send it to me through bearer.

I think that whiskey will also help, but I do not know yet. Please send me some gin if any.

I am lying on bed.

Yours good friend,
Fon of Bafut

CHAPTER SIX

BEEF WITH HAND LIKE MAN

Of all the animals one finds on a collecting trip the ones that
fascinate me most are, I think, members of the monkey tribe.
They are delightfully child-like, with their quick intelligence,
their uninhibited habits, their rowdy, eager, live-for-the-
moment attitude towards life, and their rather pathetic faith
in you when they have accepted you as a foster-parent.

In the Cameroons, monkeys are one of the staple items of
diet, and, as there are no enforced laws covering the number
that are shot or the season at which they are shot, it is natural
that a vast quantity of females carrying young are slaughtered.
The mother falls from the trees with the baby still clinging
tightly to her body. and in most cases the infant is unhurt.
Generally the baby is then killed and eaten with the mother;

occasionally the hunter will take it back to his village, keep it until it is adult and then eat it. But when there is an animal collector in the vicinity, of course, all these orphans end up with him, for he is generally willing to pay much more than the market price for the living animal. So, at the end of two or three months in a place like the Cameroons you generally find that you are playing foster-parent to a host of monkeys of all shapes and ages.

In Bafut, towards the end of the trip, we had seventeen monkeys (not counting apes and the more primitive members of the tribe, such as pottos and bushbabies) and they caused us endless amusement. Probably the most colourful were the patas, slender monkeys about the size of a terrier, with bright gingery red fur, soot-black faces and white shirt-fronts. In the wild state these monkeys live in the grasslands, rather than the forest, walking about like dogs in large family groups, assiduously searching the grass roots and rotten logs for insects or birds' nests, turning over stones to get worms, scorpions, spiders and other delicacies. Periodically they will stand up on their hind-legs to peer over the grass or, if the grass is too tall, they will leap straight up in the air as though they are on springs. Then, if they see anything that smacks of danger they utter loud cries of 'proup ... proup ... proup' and canter away through the grass, with a swinging stride like little red racehorses.

Our four patas lived in a large cage together, and when they were not carefully grooming each other's fur with expressions of intense concentration on their sad, black faces, they were indulging in weird sorts of Oriental dances. Patas are the only monkeys I know that really do dance. Most monkeys will, during an exuberant game, twirl round and round or jump up and down, but patas have worked out special dance sequences for themselves and, moreover, have quite an extensive repertoire. They would start by bouncing up and down on all fours like a rubber ball, all four feet leaving the ground simultan-

eously, getting faster and faster and higher and higher, until they were leaping almost two feet into the air. Then they would stop and start a new series of 'steps'. Keeping their back legs and hindquarters quite still they would swing the front of their body from side to side like a pendulum, twisting their heads from left to right as they did so. When they had done this twenty or thirty times they would launch into a new variation, which consisted of standing up stiff and straight on their hind legs, arms stretched above their heads, faces peering up at the roof of their cage, and then staggering round and round in circles until they were so dizzy that they fell backwards. This whole dance would be accompanied by a little song, the lyric of which went like this: 'Waaaaow . . . waaaaow . . . proup . . . proup . . . waaaaow . . . proup,' which was considerably more attractive and comprehensible than the average popular song sung by the average popular crooner.

The patas, of course, adored live food of any description and they felt their day was incomplete if they did not have a handful of grasshoppers apiece, or some birds' eggs, or a brace of juicy, hairy spiders. But for them the caviare of life was the larva of the palm beetle. Palm beetles are an oval insect about two inches in length, which are very common in the Cameroons. They lay their eggs in rotting tree-trunks, but show a marked preference for the soft, fibrous interior of the palm trees. Here, in a moist, soft bed of food, the egg hatches out and the grub soon grows into a livid white, maggot-like creature about three inches long and as thick as your thumb. These fat, twitching grubs were considered by the patas to be the Food of the Gods, and the shrieks of delight that would greet my appearance with a tinful of them would be almost deafening. The curious thing was that, although they adored eating the larvae, they were really scared of them. After I had emptied the grubs on the floor of the cage, the patas would squat round the pile, still screaming with pleasure, and keep touching the delicacies with trembling, tentative fingers. If the grubs moved, they would hastily withdraw their hands and wipe them hurriedly on their fur. At last one of them would grab a fat larva and, screwing up his face and closing his eyes tightly, he would stuff the end into his mouth and bite hard. The larva, of course, would respond to this unkind decapitation with a frantic dying wriggle and the patas would drop it hastily, wipe his hands again and, still sitting with tightly closed eyes and screwed-up face, would munch on the morsel he had bitten off. They reminded me of débutantes being introduced to their first fresh oysters.

Unwittingly one day – under the impression that I was doing them a kindness – I caused pandemonium in the patas cage. An army of local children kept us supplied with live food for the animals and they would arrive just after dawn with calabashes full of snails, birds' eggs, beetle-larvae, grasshoppers, spiders, tiny hairless rats and other strange food that our animals enjoyed. On this particular morning one lad brought in, as well as his normal offering of snails and palm beetle larvae, the larvae of two Goliath beetles. Goliath beetles are the biggest beetles in the world – an adult measures six inches in length and four inches across the back – so it goes without saying that the larvae were monsters. They were also about six inches long, and as thick as my wrist. They were the same horrid unhealthy white as the palm beetle larvae, but they were much fatter, and their skin was wrinkled and folded and tucked like an eiderdown. They had flat, nut-brown heads the size of a shilling, with great curved jaws that could give you quite a pinch if you handled them incautiously. I was very pleased with these monstrous, bloated maggots, for I felt that, since the patas liked palm beetle larvae so much, their delight would know no bounds when they set eyes on these gigantic tit-bits. So I put the Goliath larvae in the usual tin with the other grubs and went to give them to the patas as a light snack before they had their breakfast.

As soon as they saw the familiar tin on the horizon the patas started to dance up and down excitedly, crying, 'proup ... proup'. As I was opening the door they sat down in a circle, their little black faces wearing a worried expression, their hands held out beseechingly. I pushed the tin through the door and tipped it up so that the two Goliath larvae fell on to the floor of the cage with a soggy thud, where they lay unmoving. To say that the patas were surprised is an understatement; they uttered faint squeaks of astonishment and shuffled backwards on their bottoms, surveying these barrage-balloons of larvae with a horrified mistrust. They watched them narrowly for a minute or so, but as there was no sign of movement from the larvae, they gradually became braver, and shuffled closer to examine this curious phenomenon more minutely. Then, having studied the grubs from every possible angle, one of the monkeys, greatly daring, put out a hand and prodded a grub with a tentative forefinger. The grub, who had been lying on his back in a sort of trance, woke up at once, gave a convulsive wriggle and rolled over majestically on to his tummy. The effect of this movement on the patas was tremendous. Uttering wild screams of fear they fled in a body to the farthest corner of the cage, where they indulged in a disgracefully cowardly scrimmage, vaguely reminiscent of the Eton wall-game, each one doing his best to get into the extreme corner of the cage, behind all his companions. Then the grub, after pondering for a few seconds, started to drag his bloated body laboriously across the floor towards them. At this the patas showed such symptoms of collective hysteria that I was forced to intervene and remove the grubs. I put them in Ticky the black-footed mongoose's cage, and she, who was not afraid of anything, disposed of them in four snaps and two gulps. But the poor patas were in a twittering state of nerves for the rest of the day and ever after that, when they saw me coming with the beetle larvae tin, they would retreat hurriedly to the back of the cage until they were sure that the tin contained nothing more harmful or horrifying than palm-beetle larvae.

One of our favourite characters in the monkey collection was a half-grown female baboon called Georgina. She was a creature of tremendous personality and with a wicked sense of humour. She had been hand-reared by an African who had kept her as a sort of pet-cum-watchdog, and we had purchased her for the magnificent sum of ten shillings. Georgina was, of course, perfectly tame and wore a belt round her waist, to which was attached a long rope; and every day she was taken out and tied to one of the trees in the compound below the Rest House. For the first couple of days we tied her up fairly near the gate leading into the compound, through which came a steady stream of hunters, old ladies selling eggs and hordes of children with insects and snails for sale. We thought that this constant procession of humanity would keep Georgina occupied and amused. It certainly did, but not in the way we intended. She very soon discovered that she could go to the end of her rope and crouch down out of sight behind the hibiscus hedge, just near the gate. Then, when some poor unsuspecting African came into the compound, she would leap out of her ambush, embrace him round the legs while at the same time uttering such a blood-curdling scream as to make even the staunchest nerves falter and break.

Her first successful ambuscade was perpetrated on an old hunter who, clad in his best robe, was bringing a calabash full of rats to us. He had approached the Rest House slowly and with great dignity, as befitted one who was bringing such rare creatures for sale, but his aristocratic poise was rudely shattered as he came through the gate. Feeling his legs seized in Georgina's iron grasp, and hearing her terrifying scream, he dropped his calabash of rats, which promptly broke so that they all escaped, leaped straight up in the air with a roar of fright and fled down the road in a very undignified manner and at a speed quite remarkable for one of his age. It cost me three packets of cigarettes and considerable tact to soothe his ruffled feelings. Georgina, meanwhile, sat there looking as if butter would not melt in her mouth and, as I scolded her, merely raised her eyebrows, displaying her pale pinkish eyelids in an expression of innocent astonishment.

Her next victim was a handsome sixteen-year-old girl who had brought a calabash full of snails. The girl, however, was almost as quick in her reactions as Georgina. She saw the baboon out of the corner of her eye, just as Georgina made her leap. The girl sprang away with a squeak of fear and Georgina, instead of getting a grip on her legs, merely managed to fasten on to the trailing corner of her sarong. The baboon gave a sharp tug and the sarong came away in her hairy paw, leaving the unfortunate damsel as naked as the day she was born. Georgina, screaming with excitement, immediately put the sarong over her head like a shawl and sat chattering happily to herself, while the poor girl, overcome with embarrassment, backed into the hibiscus hedge endeavouring to cover all the vital portions of her anatomy with her hands. Bob, who happened to witness this incident with me, needed no encouragement whatever to volunteer to go down into the compound, retrieve the sarong and return it to the damsel.

So far Georgina had had the best of these skirmishes, but the next morning she overplayed her hand. A dear old lady, weighing about fourteen stone, came waddling and wheezing up to the Rest House gate, balancing carefully on her head a kerosene tin full of groundnut oil, which she was hoping to sell to Phillip the cook. Phillip, having spotted the old lady, rushed out of the kitchen to warn her about Georgina, but he arrived on the scene too late. Georgina lept from behind the hedge with the stealth of a leopard and threw her arms round the old lady's fat legs, uttering her frightening war-cry as she did so. The poor old lady was far too fat to jump and run as the other victims had, so she remained rooted to the spot, uttering screams that for quality and quantity closely rivalled the sounds Georgina was producing. While they indulged in this cacophonous duet, the kerosene tin wobbled precariously on the old lady's head. Phillip came clumping across the compound on his enormous feet, roaring hoarse instructions to the old lady, none of which she appeared to obey or even hear. When he reached the scene of the battle, Phillip, in his excitement, did a very silly thing. Instead of confining his attention to the tin on the old lady's head, he concentrated on her other end, and seizing Georgina attempted to pull her away. Georgina, however, was not going to be deprived of such a plump and prosperous victim so easily and, screaming indignantly, she clung on like a limpet. Phillip, holding the baboon round the waist, tugged with all his might. The old lady's vast bulk quivered like a mighty tree on the point of falling and the kerosene tin on her head gave up the unequal struggle with the laws of gravity and fell to the ground with a crash. A wave of oil leapt into the air as the tin struck the ground and covered the three protagonists in a golden, glutinous waterfall. Georgina, startled by this new, cowardly and possibly dangerous form of warfare, gave a grunt of fright, let go of the old lady's legs and retreated to the full stretch of her rope, where she sat down and endeavoured to rid her fur of the sticky oil. Phillip stood there looking as though he was slowly melting from the waist down, and the front of the old lady's sarong was equally sodden.

'Wah!' roared Phillip, ferociously, 'you *stupid* woman, why you throw dis oil for ground?'

'Foolish man,' screamed the old lady, equally indignant, 'dis beef come for bite me, how I go do?'

'Dis monkey no go bite you, blurry fool, na tame one,' roared Phillip, 'and now look dis my clothes done spoil . . . na your fault dis.'

'No be my fault, no be my fault,' screeched the old lady, her impressive bulk quivering like a dusky volcano, 'na your own fault, bushman, an' all my dress do spoil, all dis my oil done throw for ground.'

'Blurry foolish woman,' blared Phillip, 'you be bush-woman, you done throw dis oil for ground for no cause . . . all dis my clothes done ruin.'

He stamped his large foot in irritation with the unfortunate result that it landed in the pool of oil and splashed over the front of the old lady's already dripping sarong. Giving a scream like a descending bomb the old lady stood there quivering as if she would burst. Then she found her voice. She only uttered one word, but I knew that this was the time to intervene.

'Ibo!' she hissed malevolently.

Phillip reeled before this insult. The Ibos are a Nigerian tribe whom the Cameroonians regard with horror and loathing, and to call someone in the Cameroons an Ibo is the deadliest insult you can offer. Before Phillip could collect his wits and do something violent to the old lady, I intervened. I soothed the good lady, gave her compensation for her sarong and lost oil, and then somewhat mollified the still simmering Phillip by promising to give him a new pair of shorts, socks and a shirt out of my own wardrobe. Then I untied the glutinous Georgina, and removed her to a place where she could not perform any more expensive attacks on the local population.

But Georgina had not finished yet. Unfortunately I tied her up under the lower verandah, close to a room which we used as a bathroom. In it was a large, circular red plastic bowl which was prepared each evening so that we could wash the sweat and dirt of the day's work from our bodies. The difficulty of bathing in this plastic bowl was that it was a shade too small. To recline in the warm water and enjoy it you were forced to leave your feet and legs outside, as it were, resting on a wooden box. As the bowl was slippery it generally required a considerable effort to rise from this reclining position to reach the soap or the towel or some other necessity. This bath was not the most comfortable in the world, but it was the best we could do in the circumstance.

Sophie adored her bath, and would spend far longer than anyone else over it, lying back luxuriously in the warm water, smoking a cigarette and reading a book by the light of a tiny hurricane lantern. On this particular night her ablutions were not so prolonged. The battle of the bathroom commenced with one of the staff coming and saying, in the conspiratorial manner they always seemed to adopt, 'Barf ready, madam.' Sophie got her book and her tin of cigarettes and wandered down to the bathroom. She found it already occupied by Georgina, who had discovered that the length of her rope and the position in which I had tied her allowed her access to this interesting room. She was sitting by the bath dipping the towel in the water, uttering little throaty cries of satisfaction. Sophie shooed her out, called for a new towel and then, closing the door, she undressed and lowered herself into the warm water.

Unfortunately, as she soon discovered, Sophie had not shut the door properly. Georgina had never seen anyone bathe before and she was not going to let such a unique opportunity pass without taking full advantage of it. She hurled herself against the door and threw it wide open. Sophie now found herself in a predicament: she was so tightly wedged in the bath that she could not get out and shut the door without considerable difficulty, and yet to lie there with the door open was out of the question. With a great effort she leaned out of the bath and reached for her clothes which she had fortunately placed near by. Georgina, seeing this, decided that it represented the beginnings of a promising game and jumping forward she clasped Sophie's clothes to her hairy bosom and ran outside with them. This left only the towel. Struggling out of the bath Sophie draped herself in this inadequate covering and, after making sure that no one was around, went outside to try and retrieve her garments. Georgina, finding that Sophie was entering into the spirit of the game, gave a chattering cry of delight and as Sophie made a dart at her she ran back into the bathroom and hurriedly put Sophie's clothes in the bath. Taking Sophie's cry of horror to be encouragement she then seized the tin of cigarettes and put that in the bath too, presumably to see if it would float. It sank, and forty-odd cigarettes floated dismally to the surface. Then, in order to leave no stone unturned in her efforts to give Sophie pleasure, Georgina tipped all the water out of the bath. Attracted by the uproar I appeared on the scene just in time to see Georgina leap nimbly into the bath and start to jump up and down on the mass of sodden cigarettes and clothes, rather after the manner of a wine-treader. It took some considerable time to remove the excited baboon, get Sophie fresh bath water, cigarettes and clothing, by which time the dinner was cold. So Georgina was responsible for a really exhilarating evening.

But of all our monkey family, it was the apes, I think, that gave us the most pleasure and amusement. The first one we obtained was a baby male who arrived one morning, reclining in the arms of a hunter, with such an expression of sneering aristocracy on his small, wrinkled face that one got the impression he was employing the hunter to carry him about, in the manner of an Eastern potentate. He sat quietly on the Rest House steps watching us with intelligent, scornful brown eyes, while the hunter and I bargained over him, rather as though this sordid wrangling over money was acutely distasteful to a chimpanzee of his upbringing and background. When the bargain had been struck and the filthy lucre had changed hands, this simian aristocrat took my hand condescendingly and walked into our living-room, peering about him with an air of ill-concealed disgust, like a duke visiting the kitchen of a sick retainer, determined to be democratic however unsavoury the task. He sat on the table and accepted our humble offering of a banana with the air of one who is weary of the honours that have been bestowed upon him throughout life. Then and there we decided that he must have a name befitting such a blue-blooded primate, so we christened him Cholmondeley St John, pronounced, of course, Chumley Sinjun. Later, when we got to know him better, he allowed us to become quite familiar with him and call him Chum, or sometimes, in moments of stress, 'you bloody ape', but this latter term always made us feel as though we were committing *lèse-majesté*.

We built Chumley a cage (to which he took grave exception) and only allowed him out at set times during the day, when we could keep an eye on him. First thing in the morning, for example, he was let out of his cage, and accompanied a member of the staff into our bedroom with the morning tea. He would gallop across the floor and leap into bed with me, give me a wet and hurried kiss as greeting and then, with grunts and staccato cries of 'Ah! Ah!' he would watch the tea tray put in position and examine it carefully to make sure that his cup (a large tin one for durability) was there. Then he would sit back and watch me carefully while I put milk, tea and sugar (five spoons) into his mug, and then take it from me with twitching, excited hands, bury his face in it and with a noise like a very large bath running out, start to drink. He would not even pause for breath, but the mug would be lifted higher and higher, until it was upside down over his face. Then there was a long pause as he waited for the delicious, semi-melted sugar to slide down into his open mouth. Having made quite sure that there was no sugar left at the bottom, he would sigh deeply, belch in a reflective manner and hand the mug back to me in the vague hopes that I would refill it. Having made quite sure that this wish was not going to be fulfilled, he would watch me drink my tea, and then set about the task of entertaining me.

There were several games he had invented for my benefit and all of them were exhausting to take part in at that hour of the morning. To begin with he would prowl down to the end of the bed and squat there, giving me surreptitious glances to make sure I was watching. Then he would insert a cold hand under the bedclothes and grab my toes. I was then supposed to lean forward with a roar of pretended rage, and he would leap off the bed and run to the other side of the room, watching me over his shoulder with a wicked expression of delight in his brown eyes. When I tired of this game I would pretend to be asleep, and he would then walk slowly and cautiously down the bed and peer into my face for a few seconds. Then he would shoot out a long arm, pull a handful of my hair and rush down to the bottom of the bed before I could catch him. If I did succeed in grabbing him, I would put my hands round his neck and tickle his collar bones, while he wriggled and squirmed, opening his mouth wide and drawing back his lips to display a vast acreage of pink gum and white teeth, giggling hysterically like a child.

Our second acquisition was a large five-year-old chimp called Minnie. A Dutch farmer turned up one day and said that he was willing to sell us Minnie, as he was soon due to go on leave and did not want to leave the animal to the tender mercies of his staff. We could have Minnie if we went and fetched her. As the Dutchman's farm was fifty miles away at a place called Santa, we arranged to go there in the Fon's Land-Rover, see the chimp and, if she proved healthy, buy her and bring her back to Bafut. So, taking a large crate with us, we set off very early one morning, thinking we would be back with the chimp in time for a late lunch.

To reach Santa we had to drive out of the valley in which Bafut lay, climb the great Bemenda escarpment (an almost sheer three-hundred-foot cliff) and then drive on into the range of mountains that lay beyond it. The landscape was white with heavy morning mist which, waiting for the sun to drag it into the sky in great toppling columns, lay placidly in the valleys like pools of milk, out of which rose the peaks of hills and escarpments like strange islands in a pallid sea. As we moved higher into the mountains we drove more slowly, for here the slight dawn wind, in frail spasmodic gusts, rolled and pushed these great banks of mist so that they swirled and poured across the road like enormous pale amoebas, and we would suddenly round a corner and find ourselves deep in the belly of a mist bank, visibility cut down to a few yards. At one point, as we edged our way through a bank of mist, there appeared in front of us what seemed, at first sight, to be a pair of elephant tusks. We shuddered to a halt, and out of the mist loomed a herd of the long-horned Fulani cattle which surrounded us in a tight wedge, peering through the Land-Rover windows with serious interest. They were huge, beautiful beasts of a dark chocolate brown, with enormous melting eyes and a massive spread of white horns, sometimes as much as five feet from tip to tip. They pressed closely around us, their warm breath pouring from their nostrils in white clouds, the sweet cattle smell of their bodies heavy in the cold air, while the guide cow's bell tinkled pleasantly with each movement of her head. We sat and surveyed each other for a few minutes and then there was a sharp whistle and a harsh cry as the herdsman appeared out of the mist, a typical Fulani, tall and slender with fine-boned features and a straight nose, somewhat resembling an ancient Egyptian mural.

'Iseeya, my friend,' I called.

'Morning, Masa,' he answered, grinning and slapping the dewy flank of an enormous cow.

'Na your cow dis?'

'Yes, sah, na ma own.'

'Which side you take um?'

'For Bemenda, sah, for market.'

'You fit move um so we go pass?'

'Yes, sah, yes, sah, I go move um,' he grinned and with loud shouts he urged the cows onwards into the mist, dancing from one to the other and beating a light tattoo on their flanks with his bamboo walking-stick. The great beasts moved off into the mist, giving deep, contented bellows, the guide cow's bell tinkling pleasantly.

'Thank you, my friend, walka good,' I called after the tall herdsman.

'Tank you, Masa, tank you,' came his voice out of the mist, against a background of deep, bassoon-like cow calls.

By the time we reached Santa the sun was up and the mountains had changed to golden-green, their flanks still striped here and there with tenacious streaks of mist. We reached the Dutchman's house to find that he had been unexpectedly called away. However, Minnie was there and she was the purpose of our visit. She lived, we discovered, in a large circular enclosure that the Dutchman had built for her, surrounded by a tallish wall and furnished simply but effectively with four dead trees, planted upright in cement, and a small wooden house with a swing door. One gained access to this enclosure by lowering a form of drawbridge in the wall which allowed one to cross the dry moat that surrounded Minnie's abode.

Minnie was a large, well-built chimp about three feet six in height, and she sat in the branches of one of her trees and surveyed us with an amiable if slightly vacuous expression. We regarded each other silently for about ten minutes, while I endeavoured to assess her personality. Although the Dutchman had assured me that she was perfectly tame, I had had enough experience to know that even the tamest chimp, if it takes a dislike to you, can be a nasty creature to have a rough and tumble with, and Minnie, though not very tall, had an impressive bulk.

Presently I lowered the drawbridge and went into the enclosure, armed with a large bunch of bananas with which I hoped to purchase my escape if my estimation of her character was faulty. I sat on the ground, the bananas on my lap, and waited for Minnie to make the first overtures. She sat in the tree watching me with interest, thoughtfully slapping her rotund tummy with her large hands. Then, having decided that I was harmless, she climbed down from the tree and loped over to where I sat. She squatted down about a yard away and held out a hand to me. Solemnly I shook it. Then I, in turn, held out a banana which she accepted and ate, with small grunts of satisfaction.

Within half an hour she had eaten all the bananas and we had established some sort of friendship: that is to say, we played pat-a-cake, we chased each other round her compound and in and out of her hut, and we climbed one of the trees together. At this point I thought it was a suitable moment to introduce the crate into the compound. We carried it in, placed it on the grass with its lid and allowed Minnie plenty of time to examine it and decide it to be harmless. The problem now was to get Minnie into the crate without, firstly, frightening her too much and, secondly, getting bitten. As she had never in her life been confined in a box or small cage I could see that the whole operation presented difficulties, especially as her owner was not there to lend his authority to the manoeuvre.

So, for three and a half hours I endeavoured, by example, to show Minnie that the crate was harmless. I sat in it, lay in it, jumped about on top of it, even crawled round with it on my back like a curiously shaped tortoise. Minnie enjoyed my efforts to amuse her immensely, but she still treated the crate with a certain reserve. The trouble was that I realized I should only have one opportunity to trap her, for if I messed it up the first time and she realized what I was trying to do, no amount of coaxing or cajoling would induce her to come anywhere near the crate. Slowly but surely she had to be lured to the crate so that I could tip it over on top of her. So, after another three-quarters of an hour of concentrated and exhausting effort, I had got her to sit in front of the upturned crate and take bananas from inside it. Then came the great moment.

I baited the box with a particularly succulent bunch of bananas and then sat myself behind it, eating a banana myself and looking around the landscape nonchalantly, as though nothing could be farther from my mind than the thought of trapping chimpanzees. Minnie edged forward, darting surreptitious glances at me. Presently she was squatting close by

the box, examining the bananas with greedy eyes. She gave me a quick glance and then, as I seemed preoccupied with my fruit, she leant forward and her head and shoulders disappeared inside the crate. I hurled my weight against the back of the box so that it toppled over her, and then jumped up and sat heavily on top so that she could not bounce it off. Bob rushed into the compound and added his weight and then, with infinite caution, we edged the lid underneath the crate, turned the whole thing over and nailed the lid in place, while Minnie sat surveying me malevolently through a knot hole and plaintively crying 'Ooo . . . Oooo . . . Oooo,' as if shocked to the core by my perfidy. Wiping the sweat from my face and lighting a much-needed cigarette, I glanced at my watch. It had taken four and a quarter hours to catch Minnie; I reflected that it could not have taken much longer if she had been a wild chimpanzee leaping about in the forest. A little tired, we loaded her on to the Land-Rover and set out for Bafut again.

At Bafut, we had already constructed a large cage out of Dexion for Minnie. It was not, of course, anywhere near as big as the one she was used to, but big enough to prevent her feeling too confined to begin with. Later she would have to get used to quite a small crate for the voyage home, but after all her customary freedom I wanted to break her gradually to the idea of being closely confined. When we put her into her new cage she explored it thoroughly with grunts of approval, banging the wire with her hands and swinging on the perches to see how strong they were. Then we gave her a big box of mixed fruit and a large white plastic bowl full of milk, which she greeted with hoots of delight.

The Fon had been very interested to hear that we were getting Minnie, for he had never seen a large, live chimpanzee before. So that evening I sent him a note inviting him to come over for a drink and to view the ape. He arrived just after dark, wearing a green and purple robe, accompanied by six council members and his two favourite wives. After the greetings were over and we had exchanged small chat over the first drink of the evening, I took the pressure lamp and led the Fon and his retinue down the verandah to Minnie's cage which, at first sight, appeared to be empty. Only when I lifted the lamp higher we discovered Minnie was in bed. She had made a nice pile of dry banana leaves at one end of the cage and she had settled down in this, lying on her side, her cheek pillowed on one hand, with an old sack we had given her carefully draped over her body and tucked under her armpits.

'Wah!' said the Fon in astonishment, ''e sleep like man.'

'Yes, yes,' chorused the council members, ''e sleep like man.'

Minnie, disturbed by the lamplight and the voices, opened one eye to see what the disturbance was about. Seeing the Fon and his party she decided that they might well repay closer investigation, so she threw back her sacking cover carefully and waddled over to the wire.

'Wah!' said the Fon, ''e same same for man, dis beef.'

Minnie looked the Fon up and down, plainly thought that he might be inveigled into playing with her, beat a loud tattoo on the wire with her big hands. The Fon and his party retreated hurriedly.

'No de fear,' I said, 'na funning dis.'

The Fon approached cautiously, an expression of astonished delight on his face. Cautiously he leant forward and banged on the wire with the palm of his hand. Minnie, delighted, answered him with a positive fusillade of bangs, that made him jump back and then crow with laughter.

'Look 'e hand, look 'e hand,' he gasped, ''e get hand like man.'

'Yes, yes, 'e get hand same same for man,' said the councillors.

The Fon leant down and banged on the wire again and Minnie once more responded.

'She play musica with you,' I said.

'Yes, yes, na chimpanzee musica dis,' said the Fon, and went off into peals of laughter. Greatly excited by her success, Minnie ran round the cage two or three times, did a couple of backward somersaults on her perches and then came and sat in the front of the cage, seized her plastic milk bowl and placed it on her head, where it perched looking incongruously like a steel helmet. The roar of laughter that this manoeuvre provoked from the Fon and his councillors and wives caused half the village dogs to start barking.

''E get hat, 'e get hat,' gasped the Fon, doubling up with mirth.

Realizing that it was going to be almost impossible to drag the Fon away from Minnie, I called for the table, chairs and drinks to be brought out and placed on the verandah near the chimp's cage. So for half an hour the Fon sat there alternately sipping his drink and spluttering with laughter, while Minnie showed off like a veteran circus performer. Eventually, feeling somewhat tired by her performance, Minnie came and sat near the wire by the Fon, watching him with great interest as he drank, still wearing her plastic bowl helmet. The Fon beamed down at her. Then he leant forward until his face was only six inches away from Minnie's and lifted his glass.

'Shin-shin!' said the Fon.

To my complete astonishment Minnie responded by protruding her long, mobile lips and giving a prolonged raspberry of the juiciest variety.

The Fon laughed so loud and so long at this witticism that at last we were all thrown into a state of hysterical mirth by merely watching him enjoy the jest. At length, taking a grip on himself, he wiped his eyes, leant forward and blew a raspberry at Minnie. But his was a feeble amateur effort compared to the one with which Minnie responded, which echoed up and down the verandah like a machine-gun. So, for the next five minutes – until the Fon had to give up because he was laughing so much and out of breath – he and Minnie kept up a rapid crossfire of raspberries. Minnie was definitely the winner, judged by quality and quantity; also she had better breath control, so that her efforts were much more prolonged and sonorous than the Fon's.

At length the Fon left us, and we watched him walking back across the great compound, occasionally blowing raspberries at his councillors, whereupon they all doubled up with laughter. Minnie, with the air of a society hostess after an exhausting dinner party, yawned loudly and then went over and lay down on her banana-leaf bed, covered herself carefully with the sack, put her cheek on her hand and went to sleep. Presently her snores reverberated along the verandah almost as loudly as her raspberries.

PART THREE

COASTWARDS AND ZOOWARDS

MAIL BY HAND

Sir,

I have the honour most respectfully beg to submit this letter to you stating as follows:

(1) I regret extremely at your leaving me, though not for bad but for good.

(2) At this juncture, I humbly and respectfully beg that you as my kind master should leave a good record of recommendation about me which will enable your successor to know all about me.

(3) Though I have worked with several Masters I have highly appreciated your ways then all.

Therefore should the Master leave some footprints behind on my behalf, I shall price that above all my dukedoms.

I have the honour to be, Sir,
Your obedient Servent,
Phillip Onaga (Cook)

CHAPTER SEVEN

A ZOO IN OUR LUGGAGE

IT was time for us to start making preparations to leave Bafut and travel the three-hundred-odd miles down to the coast. But there was a lot to be done before we could set out on the journey. In many ways this is the most harassing and dangerous part of a collecting trip. For one thing to load your animals on to lorries and take them that distance, over roads that resemble a tank-training ground more than anything else, is in itself a major undertaking. But there are many other vital things to arrange as well. Your food supply for the voyage must be waiting for you at the port, and here again you cannot afford to make any mistakes, for you cannot take two hundred and fifty animals on board a ship for three weeks unless you have an adequate supply of food. All your cages have to be carefully inspected and any defects caused by six months' wear-and-tear have to be made good, because you cannot risk having an escape on board ship. So, cages have to be rewired, new fastenings fixed on doors, new bottoms fitted on to cages that show signs of deterioration, and a hundred and one other minor jobs.

So, taking all this into consideration, it is not surprising that you have to start making preparations for departure sometimes a month before you actually leave your base camp for the coast. Everything, it seems conspires against you. The local population, horrified at the imminent loss of such a wonderful source of revenue, redouble their hunting efforts so as to make the maximum profit before you leave, and this means that you are not only renovating old cages, but constructing new ones as fast as you can to cope with this sudden influx of creatures. The local telegraph operator undergoes what appears to be a mental breakdown, so that the vital telegrams you send and receive are incomprehensible to both you and the recipient. When you are waiting anxiously for news of your food supplies for the voyage it is not soothing to the nerves to receive a telegram which states, 'MESSAGE REPLIED REGRET CAN-NOTOB VARY GREEN BALAS WELL HALF PIPE DO?' which, after considerable trouble and expense, you get translated as: MESSAGE RECEIVED REGRET CANNOT OBTAIN VERY GREEN BANANAS WILL HALF RIPE DO?

Needless to say, the animals soon became aware that something is in the wind and try to soothe your nerves in their own particular way: those that are sick get sicker, and look at you in such a frail and anaemic way you are quite sure they will never survive the journey down to the coast; all the rarest and most irreplaceable specimens try to escape, and if successful hang around taunting you with their presence and making you waste valuable time trying to catch them again; animals that had refused to live unless supplied with special food, whether avocado pear or sweet potato, suddenly decide that they do not like this particular food any more, so frantic telegrams have to be sent cancelling the vast quantities of the delicacies you had just ordered for the voyage. Altogether this part of a collecting trip is very harassing.

The fact that we were worried and jumpy, of course, made all of us do silly things that only added to the confusion. The case of the clawed toads is an example of what I mean. Anyone might be pardoned for thinking that clawed toads were frogs at first glance. They are smallish creatures with blunt, frog-like heads and a smooth, slippery skin which is most untoad-like. Also they are almost completely aquatic, another untoad-like characteristic. To my mind they are rather dull creatures who spend ninety per cent of their time floating in the water in various abandoned attitudes, occasionally shooting to the surface to take a quick gulp of air. But, for some reason which I could never ascertain, Bob was inordinately proud of these wretched toads. We had two hundred and fifty of them and we kept them in a gigantic plastic bath on the verandah. Whenever Bob was missing, one was almost sure to find him crouched over this great cauldron of wriggling toads, an expression of pride on his face. Then came the day of the great tragedy.

The wet season had just started and the brilliant sunshine of each day was being interrupted by heavy downpours of rain; they only lasted an hour or so, but during that hour the quantity of water that fell was quite prodigious. On this particular morning Bob had been crooning over his clawed toads and when it started to rain he thought that they would be grateful if he put their bowl out in it. So he carefully carried the toads' bowl down the verandah and placed it on the top step, brilliantly positioned so that it not only received the rain itself but all the water that ran off the roof. Then he went away to do something else and forgot all about it. The rain continued to rain as if determined to uphold the Cameroons' reputation for being one of the wettest places on earth, and gradually the bowl filled up. As the water level rose so the toads rose with it until they were peering over the plastic rim. Another ten minutes of rain and, whether they wanted to or not, they were swept out of the bowl by the overflow.

My attention was drawn to this instructive sight by Bob's

moan of anguish when he discovered the catastrophe, a long-drawn howl of emotion that brought us all running from wherever we were. On the top step stood the plastic bowl, now completely empty of toads. From it the water gushed down the steps carrying Bob's precious amphibians. The steps were black with toads, slithering, hopping and rolling over and over in the water. In this Niagara of amphibians Bob, with a wild look in his eye, was leaping to and fro like an excited heron, picking up toads as fast as he could. Picking up a clawed toad is quite a feat. It is almost as difficult as trying to pick up a drop of quicksilver; apart from the fact that their bodies are incredibly slippery, the toads are very strong for their size and kick and wriggle with surprising energy. In addition their hind legs are armed with small, sharp claws and when they kick out with these muscular hind legs they are quite capable of inflicting a painful scratch. Bob, alternately moaning and cursing in anguish, was not in the calm collected mood that is necessary for catching clawed toads, and so every time he had scooped up a handful of the creatures and was bounding up the steps to return them to their bath, they would squeeze from between his fingers and fall back on to the steps, to be immediately swept downwards again by the water. In the end it took five of us three quarters of an hour to collect all the toads and put them back in their bowl, and just as we had finished and were soaked to the skin it stopped raining.

'If you must release two hundred and fifty specimens you might at least choose a fine day and an animal that is reasonably easy to pick up,' I said to Bob bitterly.

'I can't think what made me do such a silly thing,' said Bob, peering dismally into the bowl in which the toads, exhausted after their romp, hung suspended in the water, peering up at us in their normal pop-eyed, vacant way. 'I do hope they're not damaged in any way.'

'Oh, never mind about us. We can all get pneumonia galloping about in the rain, just as long as those repulsive little devils are all right. Would you like to take their temperatures?'

'You know,' said Bob frowning, and ignoring my sarcasm, 'I'm sure we've lost quite a lot . . . there doesn't seem to be anything like the number we had before.'

'Well, I'm not going to help you count them. I've been scratched enough by clawed toads to last me a lifetime. Why don't you go and change and leave them alone? If you start counting them you'll only have the whole damn lot out again.'

'Yes,' said Bob, sighing, 'I suppose you're right.'

Half an hour later I let Cholmondely St John, the chimp, out of his cage for his morning exercise, and stupidly took my eye off him for ten minutes. As soon as I heard Bob's yell, the cry of a mind driven past breaking point, I took a hasty look round and, not seeing Cholmondely St John, I knew at once that he was the cause of Bob's banshee wail. Hurrying out on to the verandah I found Bob wringing his hands in despair, while on the top step sat Cholmondely, looking so innocent that you could almost see his halo gleaming. Half-way down the steps, upside down, was the plastic bowl, and the steps below it and the compound beyond was freckled with hopping, hurrying toads.

We slithered and slipped in the red mud of the compound for an hour before the last toad was caught and put in the bowl. Then, breathing hard, Bob picked it up and in silence we made our way back to the verandah. As we reached the top step Bob's muddy shoes slipped under him and he fell, and the bowl rolled to the bottom, and for the third time the clawed toads set off joyfully into the wide world.

Cholmondely St John was responsible for another escape, but this was less strenuous and more interesting than the clawed toad incident. In the collection we had about fourteen of the very common local dormouse, a creature that closely resembled the European dormouse, except that it was a pale ash grey, and had a slightly more bushy tail. This colony of dormice lived in a cage together in perfect amity and in the evenings gave us a lot of pleasure with their acrobatic displays. There was one in particular that we could distinguish from all the others for he had a very tiny white star on his flank, like a minute cattle brand. He was a much better athlete than the others and his daring leaps and somersaults had earned our breathless admiration. Because of his circus-like abilities we had christened him Bertram.

One morning, as usual, I had let Cholmondely St John out for his constitutional and he was behaving himself in an exemplary fashion. But a moment came when I thought Jacquie was watching him, and she thought I was. Cholmondely was always on the look-out for such opportunities. When we had discovered our mistake and had gone in search of him we found we were too late. Cholmondely had amused himself by opening the doors of the dormouse sleeping-compartments and then tipping the cage over so that the unfortunate rodents, all in a deep and peaceful sleep, cascaded out on to the floor. As we arrived on the scene they were all rushing frantically for cover while Cholmondely, uttering small 'Oooo's' of delight, was galloping around trying to stamp on them. By the time the ape had been caught and chastised there was not a dormouse in sight, for they had all gone to continue their interrupted slumbers behind our rows of cages. So the entire collection had to be moved, cage by cage, so that we could recapture the dormice. The first one to break cover from behind a monkey cage was Bertram, who fled down the verandah hotly pursued by Bob. As he hurled himself at the flying rodent, I shouted a warning.

'Remember the tail . . . don't catch it by the tail . . .' I yelled. But I was too late. Seeing Bertam wriggling his fat body behind another row of cages Bob grabbed him by his tail, which was the only part of his anatomy easily grabbed. The result was disastrous. All small rodents, and particularly these dormice, have very fine skin on the tail, and if you catch hold of it and the animal pulls away the skin breaks and peels off the bone like the finger of a glove. This is such a common thing among small rodents that I am inclined to think it may be a defence mechanism, like the dropping of the tail in lizards when caught by an enemy. Bob knew this as well as I did, but in the excitement of the chase he forgot it, and so Bertram continued on his way behind the cage and Bob was left holding a fluffy tail dangling limply between finger and thumb. Eventually we unearthed Bertram and examined him. He sat plumply in the palm of my hand, panting slightly; his tail was now pink and skinless, revoltingly reminiscent of an ox-tail before it enters a stew. As usual when this happens, the animal appeared to be completely unaffected by what is the equivalent in human terms, of having all the skin suddenly ripped off one leg, leaving nothing but the bare bone and muscle. I knew from experience that eventually, deprived of skin, the tail would wither and dry, and then break off like a twig, leaving the animal none the worse off. In the case of Bertram, of course, the loss would be a little more serious as he used his tail quite extensively as a balancing organ during his acrobatics, but he was so agile I did not think he would miss it much. But, from our point of view, Bertram was now useless, for he was a damaged specimen. The only solution was to amputate his tail and let him go. This I did, and then, very sorrowfully, we put him among the thick twining stems of the bougainvillaea that grew along the verandah rail. We hoped that he would set up house in the place and perhaps entertain future travellers with his acrobatic feats when he had grown used to having no tail.

He sat on a bougainvillaea stem, clutching it tightly with his little pink paws, and looking about him through a quivering windscreen of whiskers. Then, very rapidly, and apparently with his sense of balance completely unimpaired, he jumped down on to the verandah rail, from there to the floor, and then scurried across to the line of cages against the far wall. Thinking that perhaps he was a bit bewildered I picked him up and returned him to the bougainvillaea. But as soon as I released him he did exactly the same thing again. Five times I put him in the bougainvillaea and five times he jumped to the verandah floor and made a bee-line for the cages. After that, I tired of his stupidity and carried him right down to the other end of the verandah, put him once more in the creeper and left him, thinking that this would finish the matter.

On top of the dormouse cage we kept a bundle of cotton waste which we used to change their beds when they became too unhygienic, and that evening, when I went to feed them, I decided that they could do with a clean bed. So, removing the extraordinary treasure trove that dormice like to keep in their bedrooms, I pulled out all the dirty cotton waste and prepared to replace it with clean. As I seized the bundle of waste on top of the cage, preparatory to ripping off a handful, I was suddenly and unexpectedly bitten in the thumb. It gave me a considerable shock, for not only was I not expecting it, but I also thought for a moment that it might be a snake. However, my mind was quickly set at rest for as soon as I touched the bundle of cotton waste an indignant face poked out of its depths and Bertram chittered and squeaked at me in extremely indignant terms. Considerably annoyed, I hauled him out of his cosy bed, carried him along the verandah and pushed him back into the bougainvillaea. He clung indignantly to a stem, teetering to and fro and chittering furiously. But within two hours he was back in the bundle of cotton waste.

Giving up the unequal struggle we left him there, but Bertram had not finished yet. Having beaten us into submission over the matter of accommodation, he started to work on our sympathies in another direction. In the evening, when the other dormice came out of their bedroom and discovered their food plate with squeaks of surprise and delight, Bertram would come out of his bed and crawl down the wire front of the cage. There he would hang, peering wistfully through the wire, while the other dormice nibbled their food and carried away choice bits of banana and avocado pear to hide in their beds, a curious habit that dormice have, presumably to guard against night starvation. He looked so pathetic, hanging on the wire, watching the others stagger about with their succulent titbits, that eventually we gave in, and a small plate of food was placed on top of the cage for him. At last his cunning served its purpose: it seemed silly, since we had to feed him, to let him live outside, so we caught him and put him back in the cage with the others, where he settled down again as if he had never left. It merely seemed to us that he looked a trifle more smug than before. But what other course could one adopt with an animal that refused to be released?

Gradually we got everything under control. All the cages that needed it were repaired, and each cage had a sacking curtain hung in front, which could be lowered when travelling. The poisonous snake-boxes had a double layer of fine gauze tacked over them, to prevent accidents, and their lids were screwed down. Our weird variety of equipment – ranging from mincers to generators, hypodermics to weighing machines –

was packed away in crates and nailed up securely, and netting film tents were folded together with our giant tarpaulins. Now we had only to await the fleet of lorries that was to take us down to the coast. The night before they were due to arrive the Fon came over for a farewell drink.

'Wah!' he exclaimed sadly, sipping his drink, 'I sorry too much you leave Bafut, my friend.'

'We get sorry too,' I replied honestly. 'We done have happy time here for Bafut. And we get plenty fine beef.'

'Why you no go stay here?' inquired the Fon. 'I go give you land for build one foine house, and den you go make dis your zoo here for Bafut. Den all dis European go come from Nigeria for see dis your beef.'

'Thank you, my friend. Maybe some other time I go come back for Bafut and build one house here. Na good idea dis.'

'Foine, foine,' said the Fon, holding out his glass.

Down in the road below the Rest House a group of the Fon's children were singing a plaintive Bafut song I had never heard before. Hastily I got out the recording machine, but just as I had it fixed up, the children stopped singing. The Fon watched my preparations with interest.

'You fit get Nigeria for dat machine?' he inquired.

'No, dis one for make record only, dis one no be radio.'

'Ah!' said the Fon intelligently.

'If dis your children go come for up here and sing dat song I go show you how dis machine work,' I said.

'Yes, yes, foine,' said the Fon, and roared at one of his wives who was standing outside on the dark verandah. She scuttled down the stairs and presently reappeared herding a small flock of shy, giggling children before her. I got them assembled round the microphone and then, with my fingers on the switch, looked at the Fon.

'If they sing now I go make record,' I said.

The Fon rose majestically to his feet and towered over the group of children.

'Sing,' he commanded, waving his glass of whisky at them.

Overwhelmed with shyness the children made several false starts, but gradually their confidence increased and they started to carol lustily. The Fon beat time with his whisky glass, swaying to and fro to the tune, occasionally bellowing out a few words of the song with the children. Presently, when the song came to an end he beamed down at his progeny.

'Foine, foine, drink,' he said, and as each child stood before him with cupped hands held up to their mouths he proceeded to pour a tot of almost neat whisky into their pink palms. While the Fon was doing this I wound back the tape and set the machine for playback. Then I handed the earphones to the Fon, showed him how to adjust them, and switched on.

The expressions that chased one another across the Fon's face were a treat to watch. First there was an expression of blank disbelief. He removed the headphones and looked at them suspiciously. Then he replaced them and listened with astonishment. Gradually as the song progressed a wide urchin grin of pure delight spread across his face.

'Wah! Wah! Wah!' he whispered in wonder, 'na wonderful, dis.' It was with the utmost reluctance that he relinquished the earphones so that his wives and councillors could listen as well. The room was full of exclamations of delight and the clicking of astonished fingers. The Fon insisted on singing three more songs, accompanied by his children, and then listening to the playback of each one, his delight undiminished by the repetition.

'Dis machine na wonderful,' he said at last, sipping his drink and eyeing the recorder. 'You fit buy dis kind of machine for Cameroons?'

'No, they no get um here. Sometime for Nigeria you go find um . . . maybe for Lagos,' I replied.

'Wah! Na wonderful,' he repeated dreamily.

'When I go for my country I go make dis your song for proper record, and then I go send for you so you fit put um for dis your gramophone,' I said.

'Foine, foine, my friend,' he said.

An hour later he left us, after embracing me fondly, and assuring us that he would see us in the morning before the lorries left. We were just preparing to go to bed, for we had a strenuous day ahead of us, when I heard the soft shuffle of feet on the verandah outside, and then the clapping of hands. I went to the door and there on the verandah stood Foka, one of the Fon's elder sons, who bore a remarkable resemblance to his father.

'Hallo, Foka, welcome. Come in,' I said.

He came into the room carrying a bundle under his arm, and smiled at me shyly.

'De Fon send dis for you, sah,' he said, and handed the bundle to me. Somewhat mystified, I unravelled it. Inside was a carved bamboo walking stick, a small heavily embroidered skull cap, and a set of robes in yellow and black, with a beautifully embroidered collar.

'Dis na Fon's clothes,' explained Foka. ''E send um for you. De Fon 'e tell me say dat now you be second Fon for Bafut.'

'Wah!' I exclaimed, genuinely touched. 'Na fine ting dis your father done do for me.'

Foka grinned delightedly at my obvious pleasure.

'Which side you father now. 'E done go for bed?' I asked.

'No, sah, 'e dere dere for dancing house.'

I slipped the robes over my head, adjusted my sleeves, placed the ornate little skull cap on my head, grasped the walking stick in one hand and a bottle of whisky in the other, and turned to Foka.

'I look good?' I inquired.

'Fine, sah, na fine,' he said, beaming.

'Good. Then take me to your father.'

He led me across the great, empty compound and through the maze of huts towards the dancing house, where we could heard the thud of drums and the pipe of flutes. I entered the door and paused for a moment. The band in sheer astonishment

stopped dead. There was a rustle of amazement from the
assembled company, and I could see the Fon seated at the far
end of the room, his glass arrested half-way to his mouth. I
knew what I had to do, for on many occasions I had watched
the councillors approaching the Fon to pay homage or ask a
favour. In dead silence I made my way down the length of the
dance hall, my robes, swishing round my ankles. I stopped in
front of the Fon's chair, half crouched before him and clapped
my hands three times in greeting. There was a moment's silence
and then pandemonium broke loose.

The wives and the council members screamed and hooted
with delight, the Fon, his face split in a grin of pleasure, leapt
from his chair and, seizing my elbows, pulled me to my feet and
embraced me.

'My friend, my friend, welcome, welcome,' he roared,
shaking with gusts of laughter.

'You see,' I said, spreading my arms so that the long sleeves of the robe hung down like flags, 'You, see, I be Bafut man now.'

'Na true, na true, my friend. Dis clothes na my own one. I give for you so you be Bafut man,' he crowed.

We sat down and the Fon grinned at me.

'You like dis ma clothes?' he asked.

'Yes, na fine one. Dis na fine ting you do for me, my friend,' I said.

'Good, good, now you be Fon same same for me,' he laughed.

Then his eyes fastened pensively on the bottle of whisky I had brought.

'Good,' he repeated, 'now we go drink and have happy time.' It was not until three thirty that morning that I crawled tiredly out of my robes and crept under my mosquito net.

'Did you have a good time?' inquired Jacquie sleepily from her bed.

'Yes,' I yawned. 'But it's a jolly exhausting process being Deputy Fon of Bafut.'

The next morning the lorries arrived an hour and a half before the time they had been asked to put in an appearance. This extraordinary circumstance – surely unparalleled in Cameroon history – allowed us plenty of time to load up. Loading up a collection of animals is quite an art. First of all you have to put all your equipment into the lorry. Then the animal cages are placed towards the tailboard of the vehicle, where they will get the maximum amount of air. But cages cannot be pushed in haphazardly. They have to be wedged in such a way that there are air spaces between each cage, and you have to make sure that the cages are not facing each other, or during the journey a monkey will go and push its hand through the wire of a cage opposite and get itself bitten by a civet; or an owl (merely by being an owl and peering), if placed opposite a cage of small birds, will work them into such a state of hysteria that they will probably all be dead at the end of your journey. On top of all this you must pack your cages in such a way that all the stuff that is liable to need attention *en route* is right at the back and easily accessible. By nine o'clock, the last lorry had been loaded and driven into the shade under the trees, and we could wipe the sweat from our faces and have a brief rest on the verandah. Here the Fon joined us presently.

'My friend,' he said, watching me pour out the last enormous whisky we were to enjoy together, 'I sorry too much you go. We done have happy time for Bafut, eh?'

'Very happy time, my friend.'

'Shin-shin,' said the Fon.

'Chirri-ho,' I replied.

He walked down the long flight of steps with us, and at the bottom shook hands. Then he put his hands on my shoulders and peered into my face.

'I hope you an' all dis your animal walka good, my friend,' he said, 'and arrive quick-quick for your country.'

Jacquie and I clambered up into the hot, airless interior of the lorry's cab and the engine roared to life. The Fon raised his large hand in salute, the lorry jolted forward and, trailing a cloud of red dust, we shuddered off along the road, over the golden-green hills towards the distant coast.

The trip down to the coast occupied three days, and was as unpleasant and nerve-racking as any trip with a collection of animals always is. Every few hours the lorries had to stop so that the small bird cages could be unloaded, laid along the side of the road, and their occupants allowed to feed. Without this halt the small birds would all die very quickly, for they seemed to lack the sense to feed while the lorry was in motion. Then the delicate amphibians had to be taken out in their cloth bags and dipped in a local stream every hour or so, for as we got down into the forested lowlands the heat became intense, and unless this was done they soon dried up and died. Most of the road surfaces were pitted with potholes and ruts, and as the lorries dipped and swayed and shuddered over them we sat uncomfortably in the front seats, wondering miserably what precious creature had been maimed or perhaps killed by the last bump. At one point we were overtaken by a heavy rainfall, and the road immediately turned into a sea of glutinous red mud, that sprayed up from under the lorry wheels like blood-stained porridge; then one of the lorries – an enormous four-wheel-drive Bedford – got into a skid from which the driver could not extricate himself, and ended on her side in the ditch. After an hour's digging round her wheels and laying branches so that her tyres could get a grip, we managed to get her out; and fortunately none of the animals were any the worse for their experience.

But we were filled with a sense of relief as the vehicles roared down through the banana groves to the port. Here the animals and equipment were unloaded and then stacked on the little flat-topped railway waggons used for ferrying bananas to the side of the ship. These chugged and rattled their way through half a mile of mangrove swamp and then drew up on the wooden jetty where the ship was tied up. Once more the collection was unloaded and stacked in the slings, ready to be hoisted aboard. On the ship I made my way down to the forward hatch, where the animals were to be stacked, to supervise the unloading. As the first load of animals was touching down on the deck a sailor appeared, wiping his hands on a bundle of cotton waste. He peered over the rail at the line of railway trucks, piled high with cages and, then he looked at me and grinned.

'All this lot yours, sir?' he inquired.

'Yes,' I said, 'and all that lot down on the quay.'

He went forward and peered into one of the crates.

'Blimey!' he said, 'These all animals?'

'Yes, the whole lot.'

'Blimey,' he said again, in a bemused tone of voice, 'You're the first chap I've ever met with a zoo in his luggage.'

'Yes,' I said happily, watching the next load of cages swing on board, 'and it's my own zoo, too.'

POSTCARD

Yes, bring the animals here. Don't know what the neighbours will say, but never mind. Mother very anxious to see chimps so hope you are bringing them as well. See you all soon. Much love from us all.

Margo.

CHAPTER EIGHT

ZOO IN SUBURBIA

MOST people who lived in this suburban road in Bournemouth could look out on their back gardens with pride, for each one resembled its neighbours. There were minor differences, of course: some preferred pansies to sweet peas, or hyacinths to lupins, but basically they were all the same. But anyone looking out at my sister's back garden would have been forced to admit that it was, to say the least, unconventional. In one corner stood a huge marquee, from inside which came a curious chorus of squeaks, whistles, grunts and growls. Alongside it stretched a line of Dexion cages from which glowered eagles, vultures, owls and hawks. Next to them was a large cage containing Minnie, the Chimp. On the remains of what had once been a lawn, fourteen monkeys rolled and played on long leashes, while in the garage frogs croaked, touracos called throatily, and squirrels gnawed loudly on hazel-nut shells. At all hours of the day the fascinated, horrified neighbours stood trembling behind their lace curtains and watched as my sister, my mother, Sophie, Jacquie, and I trotted to and fro through the shambles of the garden, carrying little pots of bread and milk, plates of chopped fruit or, what was worse, great hunks of gory meat or dead rats. We had, the neighbours felt, taken an unfair advantage of them. If it had been a matter of a crowing cockerel, or a barking dog, or our cat having kittens in their best flower-bed, they would have been able to cope with the situation. But the action of suddenly planting what amounted to a sizeable zoo in their midst was so unprecedented and unnerving that it took their breath away, and it was some time before they managed to rally their forces and start to complain.

In the meantime I had started on my search for a zoo in which to put my animals. The simplest thing to do, it occurred to me, was to go to the local council, inform them that I had the contents of a fine little zoo and wanted them to let me rent or purchase a suitable site for it. Since I already had the animals, it seemed to me in my innocence that they would be delighted to help. It would cost them nothing, and they would be getting what was, after all, another amenity for the town. But the Powers-that-Be had other ideas. Bournemouth is nothing if not conservative. There had never been a zoo in the town, so they did not see why there should be one now. This is what is known by local councils as progress. Firstly, they said that the animals would be dangerous; then they said they would smell; and then, searching their minds wildly for ideas, they said they had not got any land anyway.

I began to get a trifle irritable. I am never at my best when dealing with the pompous illogicalities of the official mind. But I was beginning to grow worried in the face of such complete lack of cooperation. The animals were sitting in the back garden, eating their heads off and costing me a small fortune weekly in meat and fruit. The neighbours, now thoroughly indignant that we were not conforming to pattern, kept bombarding the local health authorities with complaints, so that on an average twice a week the poor inspector was forced to come up to the house, whether he wanted to or not. The fact that he could find absolutely nothing to substantiate the wild claims of the neighbours made no difference: if he received a complaint he had to come and investigate. We always gave the poor man a cup of tea, and he grew quite fond of some of the animals, even bringing his little daughter to see them. But I was chiefly worried by the fact that winter was nearly upon us, and the animals could not be expected to survive its rigours in an unheated marquee. Then Jacquie had a brilliant idea.

'Why not let's offer them to one of the big stores in town as a Christmas show?' she suggested.

So I rang every big store in town. All of them were charming but unhelpful; they simply had not the space for such a show, however desirable. Then I telephoned the last on my list, the huge emporium owned by J. J. Allen. They, to my delight, expressed great interest and asked me to go and discuss it with them. And 'Durrell's Menagerie' came into being.

A large section of one of their basements was set aside, roomy cages were built with tastefully painted murals on the walls depicting a riot of tropical foliage, and the animals were moved out of the cold and damp which had already started, into the luxury of brilliant electric light and a constant temperature. The charge for admission just covered the food bills, and so the animals were warm, comfortable and well fed without being a drain on my resources. With this worry off my mind I could turn my attention once more to the problem of getting my zoo.

It would be wearisome to go into all the details of frustration during this period, or to make a catalogue of the number of mayors, town councillors, parks superintendents and sanitary officers I met and argued with. Suffice it to say that I felt my brain creaking at times with the effort of trying to persuade supposedly intelligent people that a zoo in any town should be considered an attraction rather than anything else. To judge by the way they reacted one would have thought I wanted to set off an atomic bomb on one of the piers.

In the meantime the animals, unaware that their fate hung in the balance, did their best to make life exciting for us. There was, for example, the day that Georgina the baboon decided that she wanted to see a little more of Bournemouth than the inside of J. J. Allen's basement. Fortunately it was a Sunday morning, so there was no one in the store: otherwise I dread to think what would have happened.

I was sipping a cup of tea, just before going down to the store and cleaning and feeding the animals, when the telephone rang. Without a care in the world I answered it.

'Is that Mr Durrell,' inquired a deep, lugubrious voice.

'Yes, speaking.'

'This is the Police 'ere, sir. One of them monkeys of yours 'as got out, and I thought I'd better let you know.'

'Good God, which one is it?' I asked.

'I don't know, sir, really. It's a big brown one. Only it looks rather fierce, sir, so I thought I'd let you know.'

'Yes, thanks very much. Where is it?'

'Well, it's in one of the windows at the moment. But I don't see as 'ow it'll stay there very long. Is it liable to bite, sir?'

'Well, it may do. Don't go near it. I'll be right down,' I said, slamming down the receiver.

I grabbed a taxi and we roared down to the centre of the town, ignoring all speed limits. After all, I reflected, we were on police business of a sort.

As I paid off the taxi the first thing that greeted my eyes was the chaos in one of the big display windows of Allens. The window had been carefully set out to exhibit some articles of bedroom furniture. There was a large bed, made up, a tall bedside light and several eiderdowns tastefully spread over the floor. At least, that was how it had been when the window dresser had finished it. Now it looked as if a tornado had hit it. The light had been overturned and had burned a large hole in one of the eiderdowns; the bedclothes had been stripped off the bed and the pillow and sheets were covered with a tasteful pattern of paw marks. On the bed itself sat Georgina, bouncing up and down happily, and making ferocious faces at a crowd of scandalized churchgoers who had gathered on the pavement outside the window. I went into the store and found two enormous constables lying in ambush behind a barricade of turkish towelling.

'Ah!' said one with relief, 'there you are, sir. We didn't like to try and catch it, see, because it didn't know us, and we thought it might make it worse, like.'

'I don't think anything could make that animal worse,' I said bitterly. 'Actually she's harmless, but she makes a hell of a row and looks fierce . . . it's all bluff, really.'

'Really?' said one of the constables, polite but unconvinced.

'I'll try and get her in the window there if I can, but if she breaks away I want you two to head her off. Don't, for the love of Allah, let her get into the china department.'

'She came through the china department already,' said one of the constables with gloomy satisfaction.

'Did she break anything?' I asked faintly.

'No, sir, luckily; she just galloped straight through. Me and Bill was chasing 'er, of course, so she didn't stop.'

'Well, don't let's let her get back in there. We may not be so lucky next time.'

By this time Jacquie and my sister Margo had arrived in another taxi, so our ranks had now swelled to five. We should, I thought, be able to cope with Georgina between us. I stationed the two constables, my sister and wife at suitable points guarding the entrance to the china department, and then went round and entered the window in which Georgina was still bouncing up and down on the ruined bed, making obscene faces at the crowd.

'Georgina,' I said in a quiet but soothing voice, 'come along then, come to Dad.'

Georgina glanced over her shoulder in surprise. She studied my face as I moved towards her, and decided that my expression belied my honeyed accents. She gathered herself and leapt through the air, over the still smouldering eiderdown, and grabbed at the top of the great rampart of turkish towelling that formed the background of the window display. This, not having been constructed to take the weight of a large baboon hurtling through the air, immediately collapsed, and Georgina fell to the ground under a cascade of many-hued towelling. She struggled madly to free herself, and just succeeded in doing so as I flung myself forward to catch her. She gave a hysterical squawk and fled out of the window into the interior of the shop. I unravelled myself from the towelling and followed her. A piercing shriek from my sister told me of Georgina's whereabouts; my sister always tends to go off like a locomotive in moments of crisis. Georgina had slipped past her and was now perched on a counter, surveying us with glittering eyes, thoroughly enjoying the game. We approached her in a grim-faced body. At the end of the counter, suspended from the ceiling, hung a Christmas decoration made out of holly, tinsel and cardboard stars. It was shaped somewhat like a chandelier, and looked, as far as Georgina was concerned, ideal for swinging. She poised herself on the end of the counter and as we ran forward she leaped up and grabbed at the decoration in a manner vaguely reminiscent of the elder Fairbanks. The decoration promptly gave way, and Georgina fell to the ground, leapt to her feet and galloped off wearing a piece of tinsel over one ear.

For the next half-hour we thundered to and fro through the deserted store, always with Georgina one jump ahead of us, as it were. She knocked down a huge pile of account books in the stationery department, paused to see if a pile of lace doilies was edible, and made a large and decorative puddle at the foot of the main staircase. Then, just as the constables were beginning to breathe rather stertorously and I was beginning to

despair of ever catching the wretched animal, Georgina made a miscalculation. Loping easily ahead of us she came upon what looked like the perfect hiding-place constructed of rolls of linoleum arranged on end. She fled between the rolls and was lost, for the rolls had been arranged in the form of a hollow square, a three-sided trap from which there was no escape. Quickly we closed in and blocked the entrance to the linoleum trap. I advanced towards her, grim-faced, and she sat there and screamed wildly, begging for mercy. As I made a lunge to grab her she ducked under my hand, and as I swung round to prevent her escape I bumped into one of the massive rolls of linoleum. Before I could stop it this toppled forward like a gigantic truncheon and hit one of the constables accurately on the top of his helmet. As the poor man staggered backwards, Georgina took one look at my face and decided that she was in need of police protection. She rushed to the still swaying constable and wrapped her arms tightly round his legs, looking over her shoulder at me and screaming. I jumped forward and grabbed her by her hairy legs and the scruff of her neck, and dragged her away from the constable's legs.

'Cor!' said the constable, in a voice of deep emotion, 'I thought I'd 'ad me chips that time.'

'Oh, she wouldn't have bitten you,' I explained, raising my voice above Georgina's harsh screams. 'She wanted you to protect her from me.'

'Cor!' said the constable again. 'Well, I'm glad *that*'s over.'

We put Georgina back in her cage, thanked the constables, cleared up the mess, cleaned and fed the animals and then went home to a well-earned rest. But for the rest of that day, every time the telephone rang I nearly jumped out of my skin.

Another animal that did his best to keep us on our toes was, of course, Cholmondely St John, the chimp. To begin with, after establishing himself in the house and getting my mother and sister well under control, he proceeded to catch a nasty chill that rapidly developed into bronchitis. Having recovered from this he was still very wheezy, and I therefore decreed that he should, for the first winter at any rate, wear clothes to keep him warm. As he lived in the house with us he already was wearing plastic pants and paper nappies, so he was used to the idea of clothes.

As soon as I had made this decision my mother, a delighted gleam in her eye, set to work, her knitting-needles clicking ferociously, and in record time had provided the ape with a variety of woolly pants and jerseys, in brilliant colours and the most complicated Fair-Isle patterns. So Cholmondely St John would loll on the window-sill of the drawing-room, nonchalantly eating an apple, clad in a different suit for each day of the week, completely ignoring the fascinated groups of local children that hung over our front gate and watched him absorbedly.

The attitude of people towards Cholmondely I found very interesting. Children, for example, did not expect him to be anything more than an animal with a curious resemblance to a human being, and with the ability to make them laugh. The adults who saw him, I'm afraid, were much less bright. On numerous occasions I was asked by apparently intelligent people whether he could talk. I always used to reply that chimps have, of course, a limited language of their own. But this is not what my questioners meant; they meant could he talk like a human being, could he discuss the political situation or the cold war, or some equally fascinating topic.

But the most extraordinary question I was ever asked about Cholmondely was asked by a middle-aged woman on the local golf-links. I used to take Cholmondely up there on fine days and let him scramble about in some pine trees, while I sat on the ground beneath, reading or writing. On this particular day Cholmondely had played for half an hour or so in the branches above me and then, growing bored, he had come down to sit on my lap and see if he could inveigle me into tickling him. Just at that moment this strange woman strode out of the gorse bushes and, on seeing Cholmondely and me, stopped short and looked at us. She displayed none of the surprise that most people evince at finding a chimpanzee in a Fair-Isle pullover occupying the golf-links. She came closer and watched Cholmondely closely as he sat on my lap. Then she turned to me and fixed me with a gimlet eye.

'Do they have souls?' she inquired.

'I don't know, madam,' I replied. 'I can't speak with any certainty for myself on that subject, so you can hardly expect me to vouch for a chimpanzee.'

'Um,' she said, and walked off. Cholmondely had that sort of effect on people.

Having Cholmondely living in the house with us was, of course, a fascinating experience. His personality and intelligence made him one of the most interesting animals I have ever kept. One of the things about him that impressed me most was his memory, which I considered quite phenomenal.

I possessed at that time a Lambretta and side-car, and I decided that, providing Cholmondely sat well in the side-car and didn't try to jump out, I would be able to take him for excursions into the countryside. The first time I introduced him to it, I took him for a round trip of the golf-links, just to see how he would behave. He sat there with the utmost decorum, watching the passing scenery with a regal air. Apart from a tendency to lean out of the side-car and try to grab any cyclist we overtook, his behaviour was exemplary. Then I drove the Lambretta down to the local garage to have her filled up with petrol. Cholmondely was as fascinated with the garage as the garage man was with Cholmondely. The ape leaned out of the side-car and carefully watched the unscrewing of the petrol tank; and the introduction of the hose and splash and gurgle of the petrol made him 'Ooo' softly to himself in astonishment.

A Lambretta can travel an incredible distance on a very small amount of petrol and, as I did not use it a great deal, about two weeks had passed before she needed filling up again. We had just come back from a local water-mill where we had been visiting Cholmondely's friend, the miller. This kind man, a great admirer of Cholmondely's, always had a brew of tea ready for us, and we would sit in a row above the weir, watching the moorhens paddling by, sipping our tea and meditating. On the way home from this tea party I noticed that the Lambretta was getting low on fuel, so we drove down to the garage.

As I was passing the time of day with the garage man, I noticed that he was gazing over my shoulder, a somewhat stupefied expression on his face. I turned round quickly to see what mischief the ape was up to. I found that Cholmondely had climbed out of the side-car on to the saddle, and was busy trying to unscrew the cap of the petrol tank. Now this was surely quite a feat of memory. Firstly, he had only seen the filling-up process once, and that had been two weeks previously. Secondly, he had remembered, out of all the various gadgets on the Lambretta, which was the correct one to open in these circumstances. I was almost as impressed as the garage man.

But the time Cholmondely impressed me most, not only with his memory but with his powers of observation, was on the occasions when I had to take him up to London, once to appear on TV and later for a lecture. My sister drove me up to London, while Cholmondely sat on my lap and watched the passing scenery with interest. About half-way to our destination I suggested that we stopped for a drink. You had to be rather careful about pubs when you had Cholmondely with you, for it was not every landlord that appreciated a chimpanzee in his private bar. Eventually we found a pub that had a homely look about it, and stopped there. To our relief, and Cholmondely's delight, we found that the woman who ran the pub was a great animal lover, and she and Cholmondely took an immediate fancy to each other. He was allowed to play catch-as-catch-can among the tables in the bar, he was stuffed with orange juice and potato crisps, he was even allowed to get up on the bar itself and do a war dance, thumping his feet and shouting 'Hoo ... Hoo ... Hoo.' In fact he and the landlady go on so well that he was very reluctant to leave the place at all. If he had been an R.A.C. inspector he would have given that pub twelve stars.

Three months later I had to take Cholmondely up for the lecture; by that time I had forgotten all about the pub in which he had had such a good time, for we had, since then, been in many other licensed establishments which had given him a warm welcome. As we drove along Cholmondely, who was sitting on my lap as usual, started to bounce up and down excitedly. I thought at first he had seen a herd of cows or a horse, animals in which he had the deepest interest, but there was not a farm animal to be seen. Cholmondely went on bouncing, faster and faster, and presently started 'Oo ... ooing' to himself. I still could not see what was exciting him. Then his 'Ooing' rose to a screaming crescendo, and he leaped about on my lap in an ecstacy of excitement, and we rounded a corner and there, a hundred yards ahead, was his favourite pub. Now this meant that he had recognized the countryside we were passing through, and had connected it with his memory of the good time he had had in the pub, a mental process which I had not come across in any other animal. Both my sister and I were so shaken by this that we were very glad to stop for a drink, and let Cholmondely renew his acquaintance with his friend the landlady, who was delighted to see him again.

In the meantime I was still continuing my struggle to find my zoo, but my chance of success seemed to recede farther and farther each day. The collection had to be moved from J. J. Allen's, of course, but here Paignton Zoo came to my rescue. With extreme kindness they allowed me to board my collection with them, on deposit, until such time as I could find a place of my own. But this, as I say, began to seem more and more unlikely. It was the old story. In the initial stages of a

project, when you need people's help most, it is never forth-coming. The only solution, if at all possible, is to go ahead and accomplish it by yourself. Then, when you have made a success of it, all the people who would not help you launch it gather round, slap you on the back and offer their assistance.

'There must be an intelligent local council *somewhere*,' said Jacquie one evening, as we pored over a map of the British Isles.

'I doubt it,' I said gloomily, 'and anyway I doubt whether I have the mental strength to cope with another round of mayors and town clerks. No, we'll just have to get a place and do it ourselves.'

'But you'll have to get their sanction,' Jacquie pointed out, 'and then there's Town and Country Planning and all that.'

I shuddered. 'What we should really do is to go to some remote island in the West Indies, or somewhere,' I said, 'where they're sensible enough not to clutter their lives with all this incredible red tape.'

Jacquie moved Cholmondely St John from the portion of the map on which he was squatting.

'What about the Channel Isles?' she asked suddenly.

'What about them?'

'Well, they're a very popular holiday resort. and they've got a wonderful climate.'

'Yes, it would be an excellent place, but we don't know anyone there,' I objected, 'and you need someone on the spot to give you advice in this sort of thing.'

'Yes,' said Jacquie, reluctantly, 'I suppose you're right.'

So, reluctantly (for the idea of starting my zoo on an island had a very strong appeal for me) we forgot about the Channel Islands. It was not until a few weeks later that I happened to be in London and was discussing my zoo project with Rupert Hart-Davis that a gleam of daylight started to appear. I confessed to Rupert that my chances of having my own zoo now seemed so slight that I was on the verge of giving up the idea altogether. I said that we had thought of the Channel Islands, but that we had no contact there to help us. Rupert sat up, and with an air of a conjurer performing a minor miracle, said he had a perfectly good contact in the Channel Islands (if only he was asked) and a man moreover who had spent his whole life in the islands and would be only too willing to help us in any way. His name was Major Fraser, and that evening I telephoned him. He did not seem to find it at all unusual that a complete stranger should ring him up and ask his advice about starting a zoo, which made me warm to him from the start. He suggested that Jacquie and I should fly across to Jersey and he would show us round the island, and give us any information he could. And this accordingly we arranged to do.

So we flew to Jersey. As the plane came in to land the island seemed like a toy continent, a patchwork of tiny fields, set in a vivid blue sea. A pleasantly carunculated rocky coastline was broken here and there with smooth stretches of beach, along which the sea creamed in ribbons. As we stepped out on to the tarmac the air seemed warmer, and the sun a little more brilliant. I felt my spirits rising.

In the car park Hugh Fraser awaited us. He was a tall, slim man, wearing a narrow-brimmed trilby tilted so far forward that the brim almost rested on his aquiline nose. His blue eyes twinkled humorously as he shepherded us into his car and drove us away from the airport. We drove through St Helier, the capital of the island, which reminded me of a sizeable English market town; it was something of a surprise to find, at a cross-roads, a policeman in a white coat and white helmet, directing the traffic. It suddenly gave the place a faintly tropical atmosphere. We drove through the town and then out along narrow roads with steep banks, where the trees leaned over and entwined branches, turning it into a green tunnel. The landscape, with its red earth and rich green grass, reminded me very much of Devon, but the landscape was a miniature one, with tiny fields, narrow valleys stuffed with trees, and small farmhouses built of the beautiful Jersey granite, which contains a million autumn tints in its surface where the sun touches it. Then we turned off the road, drove down a long drive and suddenly, before us, was Hugh's home, Les Augres Manor.

The Manor was built like an E without the centre bar; the main building was in the upright of the E, while the two cross pieces were wings of the house, ending in two massive stone arches which allowed access to the courtyard. These beautiful arches were built in about 1660 and, like the rest of the building, were of the lovely local granite. Hugh showed us round his home with obvious pride, the old granite cider-press and cowsheds, the huge walled garden, the small lake with its tattered fringe of bulrushes, the sunken water-meadows with the tiny streams trickling through them. At last we walked slowly back under the beautiful archways and into the courtyard, flooded with sunshine.

'You know, Hugh, you've got a wonderful place here,' I said.

'Yes, it is lovely . . . I think one of the loveliest Manors on the island,' said Hugh.

I turned to Jacquie. 'Wouldn't it make a wonderful place for our zoo?' I remarked.

'Yes, it would,' agreed Jacquie.

Hugh eyed me for a moment. 'Are you serious?' he inquired.

'Well, I *was* joking, but it would make a wonderful site for a zoo. Why?' I asked.

'Well,' said Hugh thoughtfully, 'I'm finding the upkeep too much for my resources, and I want to move to the mainland. Would you be interested in renting the place?'

'Would I?' I said. 'Just give me the chance.'

'Come inside, dear boy, and we'll discuss it,' said Hugh, leading the way across the courtyard.

So, after a frustrating year of struggling with councils and other local authorities, I had gone to Jersey, and within an hour of landing at the airport I had found my zoo.

THE LAST WORD

My zoo in Jersey has now been open to the public for nearly a year. We are probably the newest zoo in Europe and, I like to think, one of the nicest. We are small, of course (at the moment we have only about six hundred and fifty mammals, birds and reptiles), but we will continue to expand. Already we have on show a number of creatures which no other zoo possesses and we hope in the future when funds permit to concentrate on those species which are threatened with extinction.

Many of the animals on show are ones I collected myself. This is, as I said before, the best part of having one's own zoo; one can bring the animals back for it, watch their progress, watch them breed, go out and visit them at any hour of the day or night. This is the selfish pleasure of one's own zoo. But also I hope that, in a small way, I am interesting people in animal life and in its conservation. If I accomplish this I will consider that I have achieved something worthwhile. And if I can, later on, help even slightly towards preventing an animal from becoming extinct, I will be more than content.

ACKNOWLEDGEMENTS

BRITAIN

All the members of the expedition are very grateful to the following manufacturers who supported them in a most generous way:

S. Allcock & Co. Ltd	Fishing lines
Ashton Brothers & Co. Ltd	Bedding
Black & Decker Ltd	Drill
Bovril Ltd	Food
Brand & Co. Ltd	Food
British Bata Shoe Co.	Baseball boots
British Berkefeld Filters Ltd	Filters
British Nylon Spinners Ltd	Clothing
Cerebos Ltd	Food
Coleman Quick Lite Co. Ltd	Lighting and heating
Joseph Cookson Ltd	Rope
Cussons Sons & Co.	Toilet goods
W. M. Delf (L'pool) Ltd	Disinfectant
Electrical Equipment Co.	Generator
Ever-Ready Co. (GB) Ltd	Batteries
Joseph Farrow & Co. Ltd	Food
Granta Works	Folding canoe
Horlicks Ltd	Food
Hugon & Co. Ltd	Food
Jeyes-Ibco Sales Ltd	Disinfectant
Percy Jones (Twinlock) Ltd.	Files
G. B. Kalee Ltd	Ciné equipment
Kimberly-Clark Ltd	Tissues
Latex Upholstery Ltd	Foam rubber
Linen Thread Company Ltd	Special line
Lustraphone Ltd	Microphone

Marmite Ltd	Food
William Marples & Sons Ltd	Tools
Minnesota Mining & Manufacturing Co. Ltd	Tapes
Don S. Momand Ltd	Alka-Seltzer
The Nestlé Company Ltd	Food
Olympia Ltd	Typewriter
Oxo Ltd	Food
Pifco Ltd	Lighting
Polarisers (UK) Ltd	Sun-glasses
Prestige Group Ltd	Cooking equipment
Rael-Brook Ltd	Clothing
Reckitt & Colman Ltd	Medical supplies
Revlon	Toilet goods
Ross Ensign Ltd	Binoculars
Geo. Salter & Co. Ltd	Scales
Adhesive Tapes Ltd	Sellotape
Scott & Turner	Vitamin food
Selfset Ltd	Traps
The Sheffield Twist Drill & Steel Co. Ltd	Drills
Smiths Clocks and Watches Ltd	Watches
Spear & Jackson Ltd	Spades
Spong & Co. Ltd	Mincers
Smith & Nephew Ltd	Medical supplies
Stanley Works (GB) Ltd	Tools
Tate & Lyle Ltd	Food
Templeton Patents Ltd	Dried foods
Joseph Tetley & Co. Ltd	Tea
Tilley Lamp Co. Ltd	Lamps and heaters
United Yeast Co. Ltd	Yeast
Venesta Ltd	Plymax board
Venner Accumulators Ltd	Batteries for recorder
Vitamins Ltd	Bemax
Windolite Ltd	Windolite

Yeo Bros. Paull Ltd	Tent
S. Young & Sons (Misterton) Ltd	Animal equipment

Manufacturers whose products were of tremendous value and without which the expedition would have been seriously hampered were:

Allen & Hanburys	Entavet
Barnards Ltd	Wire netting
B.D.H.	Medical supplies
British Nylon Spinners Ltd, Pontypool	Tarpaulins, etc.
Dexion Ltd	Dexion
Glaxo Labs Ltd	Animal food
Greengate & Irwell Rubber Co. Ltd	Nylon tarpaulins
Joseph Gundry & Co. Ltd	Special nets
Halex Ltd	Plastic goods
Kenneth G. Hayes Ltd	Finch nest baskets
Hounsfield Ltd	Camp beds
Imperial Chemical (Pharmaceuticals) Ltd	Medical supplies
The Oppenheimer Casing Co. (UK) Ltd	Polythene bags
Parke-Davis & Co. Ltd	Medical supplies
William Smith (Poplar) Ltd	Tarpaulins, tent, etc.
Thomas's Ltd	Cages and special equipment
J. H. Thompson (Cutlery) Ltd	Cutlery
Transatlantic Plastics Ltd	Polythene bags
Varley Dry Accumulators Ltd	for ciné camera
Wire-Bands Ltd	Banding machine

LONDON: Mr Miles, of Grindlay's Bank Shipping Department, without whose efforts no members of the expedition would ever have arrived in the Cameroons.

ACKNOWLEDGEMENTS

CAMEROONS

VICTORIA: Mr Eric Saward, Acting Manager, U.A.C., and his wife, Sheila, who generously welcomed us to the Cameroons.

Mr MacCarney, Manager, U.A.C. who went out of his way to help us.

Mr Walker, of Elders and Fyffes Ltd, who saw that all food supplies for the animals were safely put upon the ship.

Mr Dudding, Assistant Commissioner, for all his help in arranging all our permits to catch animals.

Mr Austin, of the Agricultural Co-operative, who most kindly sent a large truck all the way up from the coast to Bafut to ensure that both we and our animals caught the ship on time.

KUMBA: Dr William Crewe, who so lavishly entertained both us and our animal cargo on our way down to the coast.

Mr Gordon, Manager, U.A.C., who supplied us with a four-wheel drive Bedford truck to take our animals down to the coast.

MAMFE: Mr John Henderson, Manager, U.A.C., for whom our gratitude knows no bounds.

Mr John Topham, who invited both us and our animals to invade his house at the dead of night and did everything he could to assist us. He also provided a truck to take the animals down to the coast.

Mr John Thrupp, District Officer of the Mamfe Division, who bore our complaints and protests with fortitude.

Mr Martin Davis, Forestry Officer, who helped us in every way and brought us Tavy, our second black-footed mongoose.

BEMENDA: Dr Paul Gebauer, of the Cameroons Baptist Mission, who, as on previous expeditions, suffered much at our hands yet always welcomed us.

ACKNOWLEDGEMENTS

Mr Brandt, Manager, U.A.C., and his wife Rona, who did everything they could to make our stay in Bemenda enjoyable.

Mr Shadock, A.D.O., who helped us in many ways to smooth our departure.

Mr Macfarlane, Veterinary Officer of the Cameroons, who gave us invaluable assistance with our animal charges.

Mr Stan Marriot, of the Agricultural Department, who recharged our camera batteries and repaired our Land-Rover on countless occasions.

Mr Dennison, Manager, U.A.C., who helped us in any way he could.

TIKO: Mr Bowerman, of C.D.C., who made all arrangements for us to stay in the Rest House prior to our sailing.

Our thanks also to the Captain, officers and men of the M.V. *Nicoya*, and in particular to Mr Terrance Huxtable, the Chief Steward, who bore with us and our animals with great fortitude and understanding.

Last of all we would like to thank our good friend, the Fon of Bafut, for giving us 'a happy time'.

ALSO BY GERALD DURRELL

THE BAFUT BEAGLES

The Bafut Beagles was the name which Gerald Durrell gave to the African enthusiasts and their mongrel dogs with whom he hunted and captured many of the oddest and most elusive creatures in the Cameroons. His adventures in pursuit of odd fauna were often as strange as the animals themselves, whose spirit and humour he captures admirably in this book.

THE DRUNKEN FOREST

Once again Gerald Durrell is in quest of the odder small birds and animals, this time in the Argentine pampas and the little-explored Chaco territory of Paraguay. For good measure he throws in a remarkable assortment of human beings.

MY FAMILY AND OTHER ANIMALS

This book is soaked in the sunshine of boyhood and of Corfu, where the author lived with his delightful family and other animals. It is crammed with amusing descriptions of quaint islanders (some of whom undertook to teach him), unforeseen incidents with livestock, and elder brothers at bay.

ENCOUNTERS WITH ANIMALS

These animals were encountered on Gerald Durrell's various zoo-collecting trips in West Africa and South America.

'Mr Durrell never has a dull moment, while there is a living thing in sight' – *The Times Literary Supplement*

Also available
Three Singles to Adventure
The Whispering Land
Menagerie Manor